THE BOOK OF JOB

THE CLASSIC BIBLE BOOKS SERIES

The Song of Solomon: Love Poetry of the Spirit
Introduced and Edited by Lawrence Boadt; Foreword by John Updike

The Hebrew Prophets: Visionaries of the Ancient World
Introduced and Edited by Lawrence Boadt; Foreword by Desmond Tutu

The Great Sayings of Jesus: Proverbs, Parables and Prayers
Introduced and Edited by John Drane; Foreword by Richard Holloway

The Gospel of St John: The Story of the Son of God
Introduced and Edited by John Drane; Foreword by Piers Paul Read

The Book of Job: Why Do the Innocent Suffer?
Introduced and Edited by Lawrence Boadt; Foreword by Alice Thomas Ellis

Stories from the Old Testament: Volume I
Introduced and Edited by Lawrence Boadt; Foreword by Monica Furlong

Stories from the Old Testament: Volume II
Introduced and Edited by Lawrence Boadt; Foreword by Morris West

Revelation: The Apocalypse of St John
Introduced and Edited by John Drane; Foreword by Richard Harries

Forthcoming

Genesis: The Book of Beginnings
Introduced and Edited by Lawrence Boadt; Foreword by Sara Maitland

The Psalms: Ancient Poetry of the Spirit
Introduced and Edited by Lawrence Boadt and F. F. Bruce;
Foreword by R. S. Thomas

Sayings of the Wise: The Legacy of King Solomon
Introduced and Edited by Lawrence Boadt; Foreword by Libby Purves

The New Testament Epistles: Early Christian Wisdom
Introduced and Edited by John Drane; Foreword by Roger McGough

THE BOOK OF JOB
Why Do the Innocent Suffer?

INTRODUCED AND EDITED BY LAWRENCE BOADT
FOREWORD BY ALICE THOMAS ELLIS

St. Martin's Griffin
New York

THE BOOK OF JOB: WHY DO THE INNOCENT SUFFER?
Copyright © Lion Publishing, 1997. All rights reserved. Printed in the
United States of America. No part of this book may be used or reproduced in any manner whatsoever without written permission except in
the case of brief quotations embodied in critical articles or reviews. For
information, address St. Martin's Press, 175 Fifth Avenue,
New York, N.Y. 10010.

ISBN 0-312-22512-1 cloth
ISBN 0-312-22107-X paperback

Library of Congress Cataloging-in-Publication Data

The book of Job : why do the innocent suffer? / foreword by Alice
    Thomas Ellis ; introduction by Lawrence Boadt.
        p.   cm. -- (The Classic Bible Series)
    Includes bibliographical references and index.
    ISBN 0-312-22107-X
    1. Bible. O.T. Job--Criticism, interpretation, etc.
I. Boadt, Lawrence. II. Series.
BS1415.2.B665 1999
223'.106--dc21

                                                    99-28745
                                                      CIP

First published in Great Britain by Lion Publishing plc, 1997.
First St. Martin's Griffin edition: September 1999
10 9 8 7 6 5 4 3 2 1

Contents

Acknowledgments

The introduction has been reprinted from *Reading the Old Testament* by Lawrence Boadt © 1984 by The Missionary Society of St Paul the Apostle in the State of New York. Used by permission of Paulist Press.

The text of 'Job in Literature' has been selected from *A Dictionary of Biblical Tradition in English Literature*, edited by David Lyle Jeffrey, copyright © 1992 by permission of Wm B. Eerdmans Publishing Co.

The unabridged text of 'Job' has been taken from the Authorised Version of the Bible (The King James Bible), the rights in which are vested in the Crown, by permission of the Crown's Patentee, Cambridge University Press.

The extract from Robert Frost has been reproduced from 'A Masque of Mercy' from THE POETRY OF ROBERT FROST, edited by Edward Connery Lathem, Copyright 1947 by Robert Frost. © 1975 by Lesley Frost Ballantine. © 1969 by Henry Holt and Co., LLC. Reprinted by permission of Henry Holt & Co., LLC.

Foreword

For those of us who are prone to what are generally known as Doubts, who are troubled by the creeping suspicion that we are, after all, alone in the universe, and are sometimes assailed by the depression which can fragment into despair, the book of Job is one of the most significant in the Bible. The words 'for now I shall sleep in the dust, and thou shalt seek me in the morning, but I shall not be' will strike a chord with anyone who has undergone the weariness of grief, the bewilderment of unspeakable pain. They are the words of a man tired beyond bearing who longs for oblivion and the end of all sensation, a man too exhausted almost to listen for an answer to his agonized questioning. From chapter 3 verse 3 to chapter 42 the book consists of a poem, a litany of sorrow touched throughout by intimations of the divine, and, being at once so human and so inspired, is one of the greatest works of art ever conceived, implicit with truth.

One of the world's earliest beliefs was that goodness and rectitude went hand in hand with greatness and prosperity, that the virtuous flourished and the wicked were cut down even in this life, and that affliction was a sign of infinite anger. Job and his friends, trained in this perspective, were at a loss to explain his misfortunes: he unaware of any wrongdoing and the comforters assuming that he must be a secret sinner and therefore have brought upon himself the wrath of God. Even today, with the examples of the gospels, the Beatitudes and the Crucifixion before us, there are some who profess to be 'biblical' Christians who cling to the same view.

The afflictions of Job began when the Lord, before whom had gathered the 'sons of God', asked Satan the 'adversary', 'Whence have you come?' and Satan answered, 'From going to and fro about the earth and walking up and down on it.' One of the most chilling reminders of ever-present evil that there could be. 'Have you considered my servant, Job...?' asks God, rather inadvisedly from a human standpoint, going on to enumerate Job's excellent qualities. Satan responds that so far Job has had nothing to complain about, being hedged about by blessings, 'But put forth thy hand now and touch all that he hath, and he will curse thee to thy face.' God, taking up the challenge, answers, 'Behold all that he has is in your power…'. Then come the disasters, thick and fast, as is often the case with disasters. Job's wife, not one of the Bible's more edifying characters, appears briefly to advise, 'Curse God and die,' and then the three 'comforters' arrive, followed by Elihu, an ambitious young person with a strong sense of himself. The faintly comic impact of the catalogue of calamity in chapters 1 and 2 is dissipated at the beginning of chapter 3 with 'Let the day perish wherein I was born…'. We turn from something rather like a provincial newspaper report to some of the most superb poetry ever written.

The three friends are on the whole upright, honourable men, originally motivated by sympathy. They grieve with Job but then begin talking, as people will, speculating on the cause of his troubles. Talk, still, possibly now under the influence of Freud and his 'talking cure', has been greatly overrated as a source of enlightenment and consolation: the speaker is too frequently carried away by his own eloquence and particular prejudice, losing sight of the point at issue. Many of the ubiquitous counsellors of our own time, our 'comforters', can be more of a nuisance than a help, seizing upon opportunities to demonstrate their skills. Eliphaz, Bildad, Zophar and Elihu are still, it seems, with us, motivated by what they perceive as a proper concern, but they are only human after all. It is not enough. People in grief sometimes need only to be left alone for a while. God seldom makes himself apparent in the midst of chatter, and God, as Job in his pain was yet aware, is the one source of consolation and the end of all our strivings, clothed in silence, the still, small voice that makes all else irrelevant.

Eliphaz, the mildest of what have now become Job's accusers, is urbane and starts politely, 'If one ventures a word with you, will you be offended?' Biblical for 'Now, don't get me wrong, but…'. He continues severely, charging that Job had only as much religion as was prompted by the prospect of reward and was moved by selfishness. He concludes that all he has said is 'for thy good'. Possibly among the most irritating words ever uttered, on a par with 'Why don't you pull yourself together?' Job answers with sorrow but undiminished faith, rebuking Eliphaz by pointing out that anyone who misuses a friend in adversity has no real love for God.

Bildad the Shuhite then has his say: he is insensitive and unjust and, as a result, cruelly provoking. He assumes that Job's children have been destroyed for their sins, a particularly hurtful suggestion since Job had been in the habit of rising early in the morning to '...offer burnt offerings according to the number of them all...', for 'it may be that my sons have sinned and cursed God in their hearts.' The death of children, no matter what the circumstances, always leaves a parent with an endless sense of guilt, which cannot have been the least of Job's sufferings. Distressed and confused as he is, he is unable to vindicate himself and pleads for a little comfort, 'Before I go whence I shall not return, even to... A land of darkness, as darkness itself; and of the shadow of death, without any order, and where the light is as darkness.'

Zophar, the third friend, takes it upon himself to insinuate that Job had behaved badly, advising, 'If iniquity be in thine hand, put it far away, and let not wickedness dwell in thy tabernacles.' Thus, he suggests, Job might be restored to his previous proud position. Job has sufficient spirit left to reply with irony, 'No doubt but ye are the people, and wisdom shall die with you.' It was common in the East to say to a man too pleased with his own intellectual attainment something on the lines of 'Oh dear, whatever shall we do when you go? All the wisdom of the world will be buried with you.' But then his brief resentment is overwhelmed by sorrow and bewilderment: 'My face is foul with weeping and on my eyelids is the shadow of death.'

Bildad returns to the attack, charging Job with impatience and presumption and continuing with a graphic description of the evils which the wicked may expect to encounter. Job, again justifiably exasperated, demands, 'How long will ye vex my soul, and break me in pieces with words?' 'Have pity upon me, have pity upon me, O ye my friends; for the hand of God hath touched me.' Not to be silenced Zophar comes back, persisting stubbornly that character determines destiny and that if Job had been a good man, disaster would not have been laid on him. Job points out what might have been evident all along: that the wicked do indeed prosper. 'How oft,' he demands, 'is the candle of the wicked put out?' It should be obvious to the meanest intelligence that in this world men are not dealt with according to merit.

Eliphaz, trying to defend the position of the three friends, ascribes to Job ill deeds in which he had manifestly no part, accusing him of exacting unjust pledges, of sending away empty the widowed and the fatherless, of stripping the naked of their clothing and of having withheld hospitality, which, in the East, would have been a virtually unpardonable offence. Even so and even now do those who have been bested in argument respond, with wild and baseless charges. We need only consider the workings of our own political establishment for illustration – a debate in Parliament or the speeches from the hustings. Job, understandably weary, longs for direct communion with God, 'Oh that I knew where to find him… Behold I go forward, but he is not there; and backward, but I cannot perceive him.' He suffers from what came to be described by St John of the Cross as the 'dark night of the soul', where God is close but hidden.

The conclusion of the book as it now stands is disappointing. Restitution in this world is not an inevitable concomitant of innocent suffering and it is neither sensible nor comforting to pretend it is so. The sense of reassurance, the curious comfort that the book of Job brings is due not to the happy ending or to *schadenfreude*, the unseemly satisfaction in the trials of another, but arises from the feeling of release derived from encountering and recognizing the perfect expression of human misery, of the malaise that can come to us all. Endurance is one of the greatest gifts of God – the faith that sustains us through the trials of mortal life, through the valley of the shadow, in the sure and certain hope of the life to come. Job cried out to God to show himself: the true conclusion of the book lies in the New Testament when our Lord came among the living and the dead. Job's faith was justified, his prayer answered.

Alice Thomas Ellis

INTRODUCTION

What is a Wisdom Book?

The wisdom writings of the Old Testament include a wide variety of books that are often overlooked by modern readers but reflect a very important side of Israel's religious faith.

The writings differ among themselves in both style and subject matter, but they all have in common certain characteristics which set them off from other biblical books:

(1) a minimum of interest in the great acts of divine salvation proclaimed by the Torah and the prophets;

(2) little interest in Israel as a nation or in its history;

(3) a questioning attitude about the problems of life: why there is suffering, inequality and death, and why the wicked prosper;

(4) a search for how to master life and understand how humans should behave before God;

(5) a great interest in the universal human experiences that affect *all* people and not just believers in Yahweh;

(6) a joy in the contemplation of creation and God as Creator.

At times, wisdom seems decidedly secular in its outlook. Many of the sayings in the book of Proverbs have no relation to faith in God at all. What atheist could not agree with Proverbs 10:4, 'Lazy hands make a person poor, while active hands bring wealth.' The same theme of secular optimism and confidence can be seen in the story of Joseph in Genesis 37–50. Indeed, Joseph never receives any word of revelation from God. He judges and acts wisely, and in the events around him he perceives the plan and wisdom of God.

These qualities appear in some degree or other throughout the Old Testament. But a few books can be specifically labelled 'wisdom' because they maintain a consistent focus on the intellectual reflection about life's problems, the quest for universal truth, the rules for life, and the nature of created reality before God. These books are:

(1) Proverbs
(2) Job
(3) Ecclesiastes (or more properly in Hebrew, Qoheleth)
(4) Ecclesiasticus (or, in Hebrew, Jesus ben Sira, or Sirach)
(5) The Wisdom of Solomon.

To these should be added the Song of Solomon (Canticles). Although it lacks the questioning-type wisdom, it values the beauty of creation and expresses confidence in human life and capacity for happiness. Certain psalms also must be classified within the wisdom literature: Psalms 1, 19:8–15, 37, 49, 73, 111, 119 and perhaps others as well. Many scholars have pointed to strong wisdom elements in the prophetic books, especially Isaiah and Amos. Both prophets use typical wisdom expressions and are concerned with knowing God's counsel or plan, but only in a general sense. Besides these, there are echoes of wisdom thinking in such passages as the Garden of Eden story in Genesis 2–3, the life of Solomon in 1 Kings 3–11, the Joseph narrative of Genesis 37–50, and the book of Daniel.

The International World of Wisdom

This special wisdom tradition is not unique to Israel. In fact, the evidence points to the opposite: Israel borrowed and learned its wisdom questions (but not its answers!) from other nations of the Ancient Near East. There are collections of proverbs from Sumeria and Babylon that date before 2000BC. Many sound like their counterparts in the book of Proverbs. A Sumerian example says, 'A chattering scribe – his guilt is great!' while Proverbs 18:13 reads, 'He who answers before listening – that is folly and shame.' Assyrian literature produced large collections of fables about trees and plants, and meditations on the sufferings of the just person and the meaning of God's justice. The most famous is the poem, 'I Will Praise the Lord of Wisdom,' in which a man tries to understand why God has punished him with suffering:

> If I walk the street, fingers are pointed at me,
> My own town looks on me as an enemy;

> My friend has become a stranger,
> In his rage my comrade denounces me.[1]

In these and other lines, the poem is so similar to the book of Job that many refer to it simply as a 'Babylonian Qoheleth', because it explores the question of *theodicy* (the problem of God's relation to the innocent person who suffers evil) so thoroughly. Since Babylonian wisdom was well established long before Israel existed, we must conclude that many biblical authors borrowed common wisdom themes when writing their own books.

Egypt also provides a large body of wisdom writings. The favoured style was a father's advice to his son on how to get ahead in life. The most famous is probably *The Instruction of the Vizier Ptah-Hotep*. In it, an ageing prime minister passes on to his successor (his 'son') the rules for success: 'If thou art one of those sitting at the table of one greater than thyself, take what he may give when it is set before thy nose!'[2] Compare this to Proverbs 23:1, 'When you sit to dine with a ruler, note well what is before you!' The much later *Instruction of Amenemopet* (8th–7th centuries BC) has many proverbs that are found in a similar form grouped as a unit in Proverbs 22:17 – 24:22. Proverbs 22:24 says, 'Do not make friends with a hot-tempered man,' while *Amenemopet* commands, 'Do not associate to thyself the heated man.'[3] While the exact relationship between *Amenemopet* and Proverbs 22–24 is not known, it seems probable either that the biblical authors had the same collection, or else that both the Egyptian and biblical writers were copying from an earlier source they both knew.

This international sharing of wisdom helps explain why Israel's wise people gave so little attention to Israel's own beliefs and dogmas. They had joined the larger and more universal search for the meaning of human life.

The Book of Job

The dramatic dialogue between Job and his three friends about the relation of suffering to human behaviour, and Job's impassioned assault on God himself, have made the book of Job one of the all-time favourite classics of world literature. Many modern playwrights, including Archibald MacLeish (*J.B.*) and Neil Simon (*God's Favourite*), have used it as the basis of successful plays. Job itself is constructed like a dramatic play:

(1)	Chapters 1–2	The scene is set with an old folk-tale about how God tested Job, who proved faithful in every case.
(2)	Chapters 3–31	A dialogue between Job and three friends, Eliphaz, Bildad and Zophar, over the meaning of divine justice and Job's suffering, ending with Job demanding that God appear and defend himself if he is a just God.
(3)	Chapters 32–37	A sudden appearance of a fourth adversary, Elihu, who challenges both the friends and Job, and demands that they submit to the divine majesty and divine control of human events.
(4)	Chapters 38–41	God himself appears and recites the power and marvels beyond human understanding that show Job's demands for justice to be arrogant. Job submits twice.
(5)	Chapter 42:7–17	The final act of the old folk-tale in which God restores Job to his greatness and attacks the friends for accusing him.

The outline shows some of the inconsistency in the book from a modern logical point of view. The folk-tale in sections 1 and 5 has nothing bad to say about Job, but condemns the friends, while the dialogue sections present the friends as defenders of God and have God himself correct Job for his pride. As a result, we can detect two quite separate sources to the book. The prose folk-tale in chapters 1–2 and 42:7–17 was an older and quite legendary story of a wise man whom God tested and found faithful. A later author, unknown to us, composed the rich and profound exploration of human innocence and suffering, divine power versus a man's search for meaning, that creates the wisdom book as we now have it. Possibly a still later author inserted the remarks of Elihu in chapters 32–37 to prepare for God's speech in chapters 38–41.

The author had the courage to move beyond simple acceptance of God's will to ask hard questions of the traditional and overconfident wisdom so often found in Proverbs and sometimes in the prophets. If God does look after the just, and does always punish the wicked, as the friends claim, why does the opposite seem to be our real experience, in which evil people prosper from their deeds and the honest person never gets ahead (Job 21:7–17)? In many ways the author is writing a parody of the smug prophets and wise teachers who assure people that everything will be all right. But the book explores a still deeper question of how one who is faithful ever comes to know God or understand his or her relationship with God. Most of Job's long speeches are concerned with either the silence of God or Job's desire for a 'right' relationship with God based on justice and mutual terms. Ultimately, the harsh reply of God destroys the hope – no one relates to God on a basis of justice or equal rights. God gives himself by means of his law and his revelation that we are to obey. For this reason, the author inserted a special poem on wisdom in chapter 28 that breaks up the dialogue but makes the firm point that no one can find the way to wisdom; only God knows it and he has given it to humans through reverent worship: 'Behold, the fear of the Lord is wisdom' (Job 28:28). But worship is also the means of knowing God face to face. As Job finally admits, 'I had only heard of you by word of mouth, but now my eye has seen you' (Job 42:5).

Job was a well-known figure of wisdom. Ezekiel suggests that he was as famed for his justice as Noah (Ezekiel 14:14, 20). Thus the use of the old folk-tale as an opening both establishes the agony of Job's situation and makes it clear that God controls what happens. This permits the author to put on Job's lips words and ideas that might shock many Israelites. The happy ending relieves the bad taste such attacks on divine goodness have created, and shows in the form of a drama how one man can grow and change his mind by learning wisdom. Other ancient peoples also explored these questions of suffering and faith. They even came up with roughly the same answer of faithful trust in the greatness of God. The Babylonian work, 'I will

Praise the Lord of Wisdom,' ends with the command, 'Creatures endowed with breath… as many as there are, glorify Marduk!'[4] The author of Job has created a version that places these fundamental human questions within Israel's belief in Yahweh. The final form most resembles the great psalms of lament with their threefold cry of human pain and lament, their call for help to God, and their promise to praise God for ever. Ultimately from the midst of doubt and questioning, Job teaches us, comes trust.

Lawrence Boadt

Notes

1. *Ancient Near Eastern Texts* 596.
2. *Ancient Near Eastern Texts* 412.
3. *Ancient Near Eastern Texts* 423.
4. *Ancient Near Eastern Texts* 437.

JOB IN LITERATURE

Characters and Quotations

Characters and Quotations

Curse God and Die

This classic counsel of despair is uttered by Job's wife in the wake of all the evils which befall him (Job 2:9). It is preceded by the question, 'Dost thou still retain thine integrity?' Her words may have been motivated by bitterness over what she and Job had endured (the Septuagint and the apocryphal Testament of Job both give her a lengthy speech in which she catalogues their degradation). Possibly she felt that blasphemy would have sudden death as a consequence, and that this would put Job out of his misery. In any case, the import of her words is to question the value of 'righteousness' (cf. Tobit 2:11–14).

Rabbinic commentary contrasts Job and Adam, the latter of whom, unlike Job, heeded his wife's bad counsel, with disastrous consequences (cf. Midrash Rabba Genesis 19:12).

As Marvin Pope observes, Job's wife was called *diaboli adjutrix* by St Augustine, and *organum Satanae* by Calvin. St John Chrysostom regarded her as a scourge by which to plague Job more acutely than by any other means (*Job*, 21–22; Anchor Bible).

Sir Balaam, the main character in Alexander Pope's *Epistle to Bathurst* – a parody of Job whom the devil tempts with riches rather than poverty – ultimately 'curses God, and dies'.

William M. Soll
Aquinas Institute of Theology, St Louis University

Devil (Satan)

The English word *devil* derives through Old English *deofol* and Latin *diabolus* from Greek *diabolos,* meaning 'slanderer' or 'false accuser'. The Greek term is the Septuagint translation of Hebrew *Satan,* 'adversary' or 'obstructer'. The devil is to be distinguished from the demons, identified in Christian tradition with the angels who followed Lucifer in his fall, and from other lesser evil spirits. The devil has been given a number of names by tradition. Most commonly he is called Satan or Lucifer, but he sometimes takes the name Beelzeboul or Beelzebub, Belial, Azazel, Mastema, Satanail, Sammael, or Semyaza, all of which derive from the Old Testament and Intertestamental literature. In modern times he also bears the name Mephistopheles. Legend and literature sometimes assign these names to different characters, usually for dramatic purposes; thus frequently in medieval and modern literature, Satan, Lucifer, Belial and others play different parts.

In the Old Testament, *Satan* was originally a common noun (e.g. 2 Samuel 19:22), but gradually it became the title of a particular being. Early biblical references picture a creature of God who prompts evil (1 Chronicles 21:1), accuses the righteous (Job 1–2), or even opposes God's will (Zechariah 3:1–2). From these passages there developed the more fully defined rebellious angel of later tradition. Two key Old Testament passages which were not originally intended to apply to the Evil One came to be associated with Satan. The serpent of Eden was not identified with the devil until the Intertestamental period (see Romans 16:20). Isaiah 14:12–15, which relates the fall of 'Lucifer, son of the morning', refers explicitly to the king of Babylon, but this passage also (and the name Lucifer) became associated with the devil during the Intertestamental period. The Isaiah passage is attached to the devil in 2 Enoch 29:4–5, in the apocalyptic Life of Adam 14:16 and apparently in Luke 10:18, but the identification was not clear and definite before the writings of Origen (AD 185–251). On the whole, the Old Testament devil is still a shadowy and inchoate figure.

In the post-exilic period, the suffering of the Jews under Greek and Roman rule prompted an intense concern with the problem of evil and the powers of evil. In 1 Enoch, 2 Enoch, Jubilees, and the Testaments of the Twelve Patriarchs, a portrait of the devil began to emerge in which he is the head of a band of evil angels in rebellion against God and enmity against humanity. The Qumran community, with its intense dualism, envisioned scenarios in which Satan led an army of evil angels and evil humans against the divine host, and the New Testament reflects similar Jewish traditions.

The temptation of Christ in the desert by Satan (Matthew 4 and Luke 4:1–13) is the most dramatic New Testament episode involving the devil, but his sinister power is referred to frequently (e.g. 1 Corinthians 7:5; Ephesians 5:10–16; 1 Peter 5:8). The essential function of the New Testament Satan is to obstruct the kingdom of God; one of his strategies is possession. Christ's exorcisms and cures are blows struck against the devil's power and signs of the imminent victory of God's kingdom over Satan (Matthew 12:22–32). The devil is 'god of this world' (2 Corinthians 4:4) but his lordship is being broken by Christ (1 Corinthians 15:20–28), a process culminating in the eschatological triumph of Christ and his elect (Romans 16:20; Revelation 12:7–12).

Patristic diabology can be best understood in the context of the struggle against Gnosticism and, later, Manicheism. The Gnostic-Manichean view combined apocalyptic diabology, Iranian dualism and Greek Orphism to produce a mythology which posited a cosmic struggle between a good God of spirit and an evil god of matter, the latter being equated with Satan. In its strongest and most coherent forms, this dualism denied monotheism and was therefore unacceptable to Judaism and the Christian community. Early patristic writings such as The Epistle of Barnabas, and works by Didymus, Hermas and St Ignatius of Antioch, show both a reaction against gnostic dualism and some influence from it, the influence manifesting itself in a doctrine of a strong dichotomy between the followers of good (often identified with the Christian community) and the followers of the devil (often identified with pagans and heretics). The power of gnostic dualism was evident still in the writings of Lactantius (circa 245–325).

The classic elements of Christian diabology, however, were established by Origen and St Augustine (354–430) and were popularized in the West by St Gregory the Great, especially in his *Moralia in Iob*. In Gregory's account, God created the angels good and gave them free will. Lucifer, one of the highest angels, sinned through pride and envy, choosing his own will over God's, and he led many of the other angels after him (these became the demons). Envious of God's love for humanity, Satan used the serpent to tempt Adam and Eve to transgress his divine ordinance. God punished fallen humanity by leaving it in the devil's power, though this power was ultimately limited by God's sovereignty. In his mercy, however, God the Father sent God the Son to liberate humanity from this slavery to Satan. The Incarnation and especially the Passion of Christ restored human freedom. Those who accept Christ form the community of the saved, 'the city of God'. Those who do not accept Christ are cut off from salvation and form 'the city of this world'. From the Incarnation until the end of the world, some will be continually added to the kingdom of God through faith in Christ; Satan continues to attempt, however vainly, to block that saving work. In the last days, Satan and the Antichrist will make a last pitched battle against the Christian community but will be foiled by the Second Coming of Christ, who will bring his kingdom to fulfillment and utterly destroy the power of Satan (cf. St Ephraim Syrus, *Nisibene Hymns; Hymns of the Nativity*).

Through the influence of Gregory the Great and the other Fathers, such views were firmly imprinted on Old English literature, most clearly in the homilies of Aelfric and the poems *Genesis B, Christ and Satan,* and in the 'harrowing of hell' narrative. These works offer a powerful extra-biblical rendering of the history of the struggle between Christ and the devil, to which further details were gradually added by folklore. Medieval theology reduced the patristic emphasis on the devil by tending to replace the ransom theory (which saw the act of salvation as God's payment of a ransom for mankind to Satan) with Anselm's satisfaction theory in *Cur Deus Homo?* (which made it a sacrifice offered by the incarnate Son to the Father and put Satan in the background), but literature on the whole preferred the more dramatic ransom theory.

The devil is a powerful figure in Langland's *Piers Plowman,* usually behind the scenes but sometimes overtly, as in his attack on the Tree of Charity in C.16 and in the harrowing of hell (B.18; C.20). Chaucer, for the most part, prefers to present the devil satirically (*Monk's Tale; Friar's Tale* and *Prologue*), an approach taken also frequently in the morality plays. His most dramatic appearances in Middle English literature are in the York, N-Town, Towneley, and Chester mystery plays, especially in the plays centred on his fall, the temptation of Adam and Eve, the Annunciation, and the harrowing of hell. Sometimes frightening in these plays, he is more often a fool, as the playwrights exploit the audience's knowledge that all of his posturings against the kingdom of God will be foiled. By the 14th century, then, the devil had, in literary treatments at least, become more often comic than fearsome. This trend was reversed, however, during the 15th to 17th centuries, the period during which Satan's power was perceived to be at its height.

The leading Protestant Reformers, especially Luther (who came to the subject with strong Germanic convictions about the existence and power of demons), returning to what they saw as a biblical emphasis upon the power of Satan, added to the new fear of the devil. The legend of Faust, homocentric, pessimistic, and individualistic, reflected this view; it also produced, in the German Faustbook of 1587, the first use of the name Mephistopheles. Marlowe's adaptation of the legend in *Doctor Faustus* (1588 or 1589) produced the first major diabolical portrait in modern English literature in the character of Mephistopheles, here Satan's agent rather than the devil himself. Spenser shows the devil in human guise (e.g., Archimago, Orgoglio) and in the form of a dragon. Shakespeare presents humans demonized by their sin (Aaron in *Titus Andronicus,* Richard in *Henry VI* (3) and *Richard III,* Angelo in *Measure for Measure,* Edmund in *King Lear,* and Iago in *Othello*), though in both *Hamlet* and *Macbeth* the devil's evil, destructive power can also be felt more directly.

Although belief in the devil's power was almost universal among both the elite and the uneducated during the early 17th century, English philosophers such as Francis Bacon (1561–1628) and John Locke (1632–1704) laid the basis for scepticism regarding both witchcraft and the devil. English writers, as a result, were divided over whether to treat the devil seriously (as in Barnabe Barnes, *The Devil's Charter,* 1607), or satirically. The comic Satan of Ben Jonson's *The Devil Is an Ass* (1616) clearly indicates Jonson's scepticism; John Webster's *The White Devil* (1608) and Thomas Middleton's *The Changeling* (1623) emphasize the evil in humanity. Sir Thomas Browne argues in *Religio Medici* (1.30, 31, 37; cf. *Pseudodoxia Epidemica,* 1.10, 11) that the denial of supernatural evil is tantamount to atheism, that the devil, being the father of lies, often seduces people into a scepticism concerning his own existence in order to pursue his diabolical ends.

John Bunyan, in his characterization of Apollyon in *The Pilgrim's Progress* (1678) and Diabolus in *The Holy War,* presents a potent Satanic presence. But the most vivid (and influential) portrait of the devil in English literature is unquestionably that by Milton in *Paradise Lost* (1667; revised 1674) and *Paradise Regained* (1671). Milton added a wealth of detail, colour, and texture to the traditional story, but the two most important effects of his poems on diabology were first to set the story in language so powerful and memorable that it was henceforth fixed in the literary imagination in Milton's terms even more than in the Bible's, and second to portray the devil's character in a 'heroic' vein. Critics still argue whether Milton made Satan more heroic than he intended; whatever one's critical position, it is undeniable that Satan, 'High on a Throne of Royal State, which far / Outshone the wealth of Ormus and of Ind', can be seen as a figure of immense majesty (*Paradise Lost* 2.1–2).

The deism and scepticism of the 18th century undermined belief in the existence of the devil, the key philosophical text being David Hume's 'Essay on Miracles', the tenth chapter of *An Enquiry concerning Human Understanding* (1748). Daniel Defoe's *The Political History of the Devil* (1726) affirms orthodox belief in the devil's existence, but his interest in the subject is not apologetic but 'aesthetic': stories about diabolical encounters are intrinsically fascinating. By the end of the century, traditional beliefs had eroded to the point that Satan could scarcely be taken even as a credible metaphor. 'Gothic' writings degraded the 'sublime' to produce horrors and thrills by portraying the grotesque, the decadent, the wild, and the monstrous. Matthew Lewis' *The Monk* (1796), Robert Maturin's *Melmoth the Wanderer* (1820), and Walter Scott's *Letters on Demonology and Witchcraft* (1830; 1884) exemplified this attitude, using demons alongside ghosts, corpses, and witches for the purpose of inducing horror.

The French Revolution acted as a catalyst for a radical revision of the concept of the devil. English writers, perceiving the Revolution as a just rebellion against a tyrant king, recharacterized Satan as an heroic rebel against the tradition and authority of the evil tyrant, God. Thus William Blake (1757–1827) reinterprets Milton's devil as a hero in the struggle against tyranny, church, and convention. Satan is good, and Jesus is satanic because he acts from feelings rather than rules and breaks the commandments out of mercy. But Blake's Satan is also evil, representing hardness of heart, insensitivity, lack of love, and obstruction of the creative processes of art. The evil of both God and Satan is underscored in *The Book of Urizen* (1794), where Urizen represents Jehovah, the blind tyrant of rules and laws; Orc struggles for liberation from Urizen's tyranny, but Orc's violence and hostility make him evil as well. On the whole Blake tends to perceive God and devil, heaven and hell, good and evil as elements of a shattered whole which seeks reunion, centring, and integration. Real evil lies in anything which obstructs that process of integration.

The Romantics perpetuate Blake's ambivalence towards the devil. Lord Byron's *Cain* (1821) asks who is the more evil – Lucifer, who gave Adam and Eve knowledge, or Jehovah, who drove them out of the Garden to exile and death? But Lucifer also is blind and self-absorbed, rejecting the only possible creative road, his integration with Jehovah. In his treatise *On the Devil and Devils* (1821), Shelley argues that Manichean dualism affords a valid insight into the divided state of the human soul. For Shelley, Milton's great insight lay in his making his God no better than his devil. In *Prometheus Unbound* (1820) Shelley recognizes the difficulty in making Satan a hero and so shifts the qualities of heroic rebellion to Prometheus, who is free of the aggressive, stingy, unloving elements which make Satan an inappropriate hero for the Romantic ethos. Meanwhile, Mary Shelley's *Frankenstein; or, The Modern Prometheus* (1818) took a great step in shifting the focus of terror from the demon to the monster and from the supernatural to science fiction, presenting a character who was made a monster by a humanity which first created and then abused him. The early Romantic experiment with making the devil a symbol of good was gradually replaced by the tendency to divorce the devil from serious discussions of good and evil. He is frequently made the subject of light or humorous stories such as Thackeray's 'The Devil's Wager' (1833) and 'The Painter's Bargain' (1834), reviving an earlier folklore motif concerning battles of wits between the devil and humans over a bargain which had been struck between them (cf. Max Beerbohm's 'Enoch Soames', 1917, Stephen V. Benét's 'The Devil and Daniel Webster', 1937, and more recent stories, some collected in Basil Davenport's *Deals with the Devil*, 1958).

In 19th-century America the tendency to centre evil in humanity rather than in the supernatural was even more pronounced than in England. For example, in stories of real horror Poe always eschewed Satan; his devil stories, such as 'The Devil in the Belfry' (1839) and 'Never Bet the Devil Your Head' (1841), are humorous. The devil appears incidentally, however, in Hawthorne's 'Young Goodman Brown' (1835) and his presence is evident in Melville's *Moby Dick* (1851) and *The Confidence-Man* (1857), the latter of which presents a demonic trickster who makes fools of the passengers on the riverboat 'Fidèle'.

The revival of the occult at the end of the 19th century produced some late Romantic sympathy for the devil (Marie Corelli, *The Sorrows of Satan,* 1895) and the explicit Satanism of Aleister Crowley, (1875–1947), but ironic treatment remained the norm, as in the 'Don Juan in Hell' section of Shaw's *Man and Superman* (1903). The attack on traditional views by Darwin, Marx, Nietzsche, and Freud had demolished the old concept and opened the door to a nihilism seen at its bleakest in Mark Twain's work on 'The Mysterious Stranger', which appeared in three main versions, the latest of which was *No. 44, The Mysterious Stranger* (1982). At its conclusion the devil announces that there 'is no God, no universe, no human race, no earthly life, no heaven, no hell. It is all a Dream, a grotesque and foolish dream.'

The horrors of the mid and late 20th century, which have contradicted liberal optimism about the essential goodness of human nature, have prompted the revival of serious treatments of the traditional devil, as in C.S. Lewis' *Screwtape Letters* (1942) and *Perelandra* (1944), Dorothy Sayers' *The Devil to Pay* (1939), and Flannery O'Connor's *The Violent Bear It Away* (1960). John Updike's *The Witches of Eastwick* affords a recent noteworthy devil-portrait, one which has also found its way into film, alongside *The Omen, The Exorcist,* and other 'popular' tales of diabolical horror.

Jeffrey Burton Russell
University of California, Santa Barbara

Dust and Ashes

Dust and ashes is a metonymic term for the human condition as conceived humbly by Abraham (Genesis 18:27) and also by Job who, in lamenting his lot, said, 'I am become like dust and ashes'

(Job 30:19), and later, when he finally was able to answer the voice of God speaking out of the whirlwind, said, 'I abhor myself, and repent in dust and ashes' (42:6).

In Christian tradition these passages are associated with discussion of repentance and the need for humility before God (e.g., St Ambrose, *De poenitentia*, 2.1.3–4). The image also has a place in the liturgy for burial of the dead, where it is conflated with Genesis 3:19, 'for dust thou art, and unto dust thou shalt return.' In this context it is cited by Washington Irving in 'The Pride of the Village' and Thomas Wolfe in *Look Homeward, Angel,* where, as Eugene's mind 'fumbled at little things' despite the nasal drone of the Presbyterian minister, 'Horse Hines bent ceremoniously, with a starched crackle of shirt, to throw his handful of dirt into the grave. "Ashes to ashes–"' (chapter 37). In the Anglican (and Episcopalian) liturgy the phrase which immediately follows is 'in sure and certain hope of the Resurrection to eternal life, through our Lord Jesus Christ', prompting Longfellow's rejoinder: '"Dust thou art, to dust returnest", / Was not spoken of the soul' ('A Psalm of Life', 2). Reflecting on the grave of his father, Dickens' narrator in *David Copperfield* considers 'the mound above the ashes and dust that once was he, without whom I had never been' (chapter 1). Hardy uses the phrase as a kind of shorthand for death (*Desperate Remedies,* chapter 21) as well as 'living death': in *Tess of the D'Urbervilles,* after Tess has been raped by Alec, Hardy says of her feelings that 'he was dust and ashes to her', and later, after her husband has left her, Tess feels that in her 'was the record of a pulsing life which had learnt too well, for its years, the dust and ashes of things'.

By natural extension the phrase was adopted for the imposition of ashes on Ash Wednesday in Anglican and Catholic Lenten liturgies. It is likely this connection which Dickens has in mind in *A Tale of Two Cities,* where his attention is turned towards the lot of one of the ordinary labourers: 'For, in these times, as the mender of roads worked, solitary, in the dust, not often troubling himself to reflect that dust he was and to dust he must return, being for the most part too much occupied in thinking how little he had for supper and how much more he would eat if he had it' (2.23). Farrell's Studs Lonigan, in *Judgment Day,* is crudely reminded of his mortality: 'Remember, O Lonigan, that thou art dirty dust, and like a dirty dog thou shalt return to dirtier dust' (chapter 17). A variant of the penitential formulation forms the title – 'Wash, this Sand and Ashes' – of the eleventh chapter in Rudy Wiebe's saga of the Mennonite diaspora, *The Blue Mountains of China*.

David L. Jeffrey
University of Ottawa

I Know That My Redeemer Liveth

Job's statement of faith *in extremis* is 'For I know that my redeemer liveth, and that he shall stand at the latter day upon the earth: And though after my skin worms destroy this body, yet in my flesh shall I see God' (Job 19:25–26). The conjectural uncertainty of the King James Version rendering of verse. 26 has not been completely solved by subsequent translations. (The translation 'skin worms destroy this body' may arise in part from a later medieval notion that one's living flesh already harbours the eggs of worms set to hatch at death and do their grisly work.)

In one of the most influential English commentaries on the passage, Matthew Henry (1728) draws attention to the Hebrew word translated Redeemer, showing that it properly indicates a 'next of kin', as in the kinsman-redeemer of the book of Ruth. He thus reads the passage as prefigurative of Christ, the 'son of Man' as 'near of kind to us, the next kinsman that is able to redeem; he has paid our debt' (*Commentary on the Whole Bible*, 3.109). These words are among the best known in the Bible, not only because of their use in funeral oration but also through their magnificent setting in Handel's *Messiah*. Hence, for a character in Mulock's *John Halifax*, as soon as the first musical phrase falls upon the ear, 'That is Handel – "I know that my Redeemer liveth." Exquisitely she played it, the clear treble notes seeming to utter like a human voice the very words...', at which the entire passage comes back, word by word, note by note (chapter 27). It is the triumphal christological note that Shaw's St Joan sounds: 'My sword shall conquer yet: The sword that never struck a blow. Though men destroyed my body, yet in my soul have I seen God' (*St Joan*, Epilogue).

David L. Jeffrey
University of Ottawa

I Only am Escaped

In Job 1, after God had permitted Satan to test Job's faith (v. 12), a series of catastrophes befell Job: his oxen and asses were stolen and their keepers slain by Arabs (vv. 14–15); his sheep and shepherds were consumed by lightning (v. 16); his camels were stolen and the servants tending them killed by Chaldeans (v. 17); and, finally, in a terrible climax, his seven sons and three daughters died when the house in which they were feasting collapsed in a storm (vv. 18–19). All of these calamities, alternately caused by human violence and natural phenomena, were reported to Job by four sole survivors in rapid succession ('While he was yet speaking, there came also another…'), each concluding his item of 'news' with the words 'and I only am escaped alone to tell thee' (vv. 15–17, 19). The parallel structure of these reports gives this concluding sentence the function of a refrain and heightens the impression of 'cruel irony' (Weiser) in the shattering sequence of events.

The Fathers suggest allegorical meanings for each of the dire messages. St Jerome sees the house (Job 1:18) as representing the Church, and the Chaldeans as symbolizing demons (*Commentarii in Job,* 1). In St Gregory the Great's view, the messengers are Satan's tools, whose words are meant to make Job believe that God is hurting him (*Moralia in Iob,* 2.14; cf. also Didymus the Blind, *Commentarii in Job*).

In English literature the messengers' refrain frequently serves to establish a narrative frame. William Blake's *The Four Zoas* (3.103) and *Jerusalem* (chapter 2, pl. 29, lines 29, 82) offer examples. Herman Melville cites the refrain for the same rhetorical purpose in *Moby Dick* (having made an earlier allusion to it in *Redburn,* chapter 59). As a motto for the novel's epilogue, the sentence finally identifies Ishmael, the narrator, as the fate-ordained sole survivor of the wreck of the *Pequod.* At the same time, it reinforces many previous allusions to the book of Job and once again takes up Ahab's notion that the evil in the world is wrought, or at least tolerated, by God.

In Archibald MacLeish's *J.B.,* two messengers announce the deaths of J.B.'s children. The Second Messenger repeatedly asserts, 'I only am escaped alone to tell thee' (scenes 3, 4, and 6). He transcends his traditional role as 'Job's post' (as Carlyle termed the carriers of bad news in *The French Revolution*, 3.3.4) and emerges as a complex and reluctant witness:

> Someone chosen by the chance of seeing,
> By the accident of sight,
> By stumbling on the moment of it,
> Unprepared, unwarned, unready,
> Thinking of nothing, of his drink, his bed,
> Caught in that inextricable net,
> His belly, and it happens, and he sees it...
> Caught in that inextricable net
> Of having witnessed, having seen...
> He alone!

Howard Nemerov's poem 'I Only Am Escaped to Tell Thee' suggests that a Victorian lady's whalebone corset is a violation of nature. Its title alludes to Melville's use of the sentence at the end of *Moby Dick*, but in its new context it also exploits the sinister overtones of the words from the original source, Job, to convey feelings of impending catastrophe.

Manfred Siebald
Johannes Gutenberg Universität, Mainz, Germany

Job

Within the Bible, Job is remembered and commended principally for his righteousness (Ezekiel 14:12–14) and patience (Tobit 2:10–23; James 5:11). The latter virtue is stressed more in the Septuagint than in the original Hebrew; Job's wife's role in the story is also expanded (2:7–9, 11), and other minor details of the plot are modified. The pseudepigraphal Testament of Job, a Greek work of the 1st century BC, alters the plot even more drastically, adding characters (serving women, physicians) and greatly expanding the roles of Satan, Job's wife, and his daughters.

In medieval Christian exegesis Job figures as a paragon of patience, an *athleticus Dei* or *miles Christi* figure, and an antitype of Christ. He appears in all these roles in St Gregory the Great's influential *Moralia in Iob,* a work heavily indebted to St Jerome (*Commentarii in librum Job: Patrologia Latina,* 26.655–850), St Ambrose (*De interpellatione Job et David: Patrologia Latina,* 14.797–850), and St Augustine (*De patientia: Patrologia Latina,* 40.615–16). Gregory's *Moralia* dominates almost all subsequent medieval treatment of the book of Job, including those of St Thomas Aquinas and Nicholas of Lyra. In light of Job 19:25–27 ('For I know that my redeemer liveth...') Gregory is typical of medieval commentators in regarding Job as a prophet of the general resurrection of the dead. Jerome, Gregory, and others discuss the verse structure of the book of Job (most think it to be in hexameters); some go further and classify it as epic or drama. Protestant exegetical tradition, as represented in Calvin (*Sermons on the Book of Job,* 1563) and Beza (*Iobus...Illustratus,* 1589), is largely consistent with that of the Middle Ages.

In the matins of the Office of the Dead (the '*Dirige*') of the High Middle Ages, nine lessons from the book of Job alternate with readings from the Psalms. Job himself has a place in medieval liturgy as patron saint of sufferers from worms, leprosy, various skin diseases, venereal disease, and melancholy.

Literary representations draw upon all of these biblical, apocryphal, and ecclesiastical sources, as well as Prudentius' influential portrait of Job in the *Psychomachia.* Job appears briefly in Cynewulf's *Ascension (Christ II),* in the Old English *Phoenix,* and in a homily by Aelfric. In the 12th century, Peter Riga's *Aurora* treats the story of Job in 576 Latin hexameters, mainly a précis of passages from the *Moralia.* Peter of Blois' prose *Compendium in Iob* (1173), also indebted to the *Moralia,* was translated into French in the late 13th century as *L'hystore Job.* In Middle English there are three different versions of a 15th-century work called *Pety Iob* (also known as *Lessons of the Dirige*), a paraphrase and elaboration of the verses from Job in the matins of the Office of the Dead. Other Middle English treatments of the Job legend include an early-15th-century verse paraphrase of the biblical narrative (indebted in places to the *Pety Iob*), and a brief late-15th-century 'Life of Job' in rhyme-royal (with affinities to the Testament of Job). In addition there are medieval Portuguese and Middle High German paraphrases of Job, a poem in Italian (circa

1495) by Giuliano Dati of Florence, and a popular 15th-century French play, *La pacience de Job*, which freely combines elements from earlier tradition.

Chaucer's Clerk (*Canterbury Tales*, 4.932–34) and Wife of Bath (3.433–36) both make reference to Job in novel, ironic contexts. Marlowe, Shakespeare, and other Elizabethans refer to Job's proverbial patience and there are, in the 17th century, a number of verse reworkings of the book of Job. The first major English author to use the narrative in an extensive way is Milton, whose *Paradise Regained* (1671) not only contains unmistakable echoes of the book of Job but is also, as Lewalski's landmark study (1966) has shown, self-consciously modelled upon it. *Samson Agonistes* also has strong affinities with the Job story.

Blake's *Illustrations of the Book of Job* (1825) occupies a pivotal place in the history of the Job story and its influence on English literature. Stressing the propriety of Job's rebellious questioning of God's justice, Blake refashioned the patient Job of earlier tradition into a romantic rebel. Shelley, who at one time apparently intended to compose a 'lyrical drama' based on the book of Job, expresses his own somewhat Blakean view of the narrative in *Prometheus Unbound* (1820). Tennyson actually learned Hebrew in order to translate the book of Job, though he never achieved his goal.

Of the many plays based on the Job story which have appeared in the 20th century, Archibald MacLeish's *J.B.* (1958) is the best known and most significant. In it Job has become a modern businessman who suffers a series of catastrophes and who finds redemption in the love of his wife and of God. Robert Frost's *Masque of Reason* (1945) is a wry dramatic poem in which the theological paradoxes of the book of Job are held up to Voltairean ridicule. I.A. Richards' *Job's Comforting* (1970) is a bitterly ironic play in verse made up of passages from the biblical narrative 're-arranged, and with a single sentence added'. In the spirit of Blake, Richards rejects the easy reconciliation of God and man at the end of the biblical story.

Since 1970 numerous short poems based on various facets of the Job story have appeared (favourite topics being the relationship between Job and his wife, and his wife's point of view on the story). Some critics find deep connections between the book of Job and absurdist drama, in particular the plays of Ionesco, Adamov, and Beckett, but the relationship may be one of analogy rather than of a source to its immediate derivatives. In either case, whether directly or indirectly, the book of Job – which Tennyson called 'the greatest poem of ancient and modern times' – continues to exert a profound influence on the literary culture of our time.

Lawrence Besserman
Hebrew University of Jerusalem

Job's Comforters

In the second chapter of Job, after Job has lost all his belongings, his family, and his health, three friends come 'to mourn with him and to comfort him'. After sitting silently with him for seven days and seven nights, they try to convince Job, in three rounds of discussion (Job 3–31), that he has deserved his misfortunes. Job's judgment in 16:2, 'miserable comforters are ye all' (literally 'comforters of trouble'), sets the tone for subsequent interpretation of them.

The eldest of the friends, Eliphaz of Teman, emphasizes man's iniquity; Bildad the Shuhite stresses God's justice, and Zophar from Naamah enlarges on God's inscrutability. In the end, after they have given up talking to Job and after a fourth man, Elihu, has continued the discussion, the friends are reproached by God for not having 'spoken the thing which is right' (42:7, 8). They are told to make a burnt offering, and God accepts Job's prayer on their behalf (42:9, 10).

Talmudic legend (Ginzberg, *Legends of the Jews*, 2.236–37; 3.356) makes the three comforters cousins of Job; all four cousins are said to be kings of lands 300 miles apart from one another and descendants of Nahor, the brother of Abraham. They each wear crowns adorned with pictures of the other three, and when adversity or misfortune comes upon one of them, the others immediately perceive alteration in the picture of that cousin.

Medieval commentary is typically less interested in the three comforters than in Job's response to them and his discussion with God. Standard medieval views on the comforters were heavily influenced by St Gregory's *Moralia in Iob*, 2.13, which presents the comforters as well intended but lacking in restraint, guilty of the reproach, 'Cursed be he that does the work of the Lord negligently' (Jeremiah 48:10). Commenting on Job 16:2, Gregory applies the point especially to the counselling of fellow Christians, observing that 'elect persons, even when they are bereft of temporal glory, do not lose the forcibleness of interior judgment', and adding that the 'windy words' of the comforters (v. 3) serve only 'the end of temporal inflating, rather than the end of righteousness'.

For Calvin, in his *Sermons on Job,* the comforters are 'like devils', torturing Job 'worse than he has been tortured before'. Though they have good intentions, they lack love and so, according to 1 Corinthians 13, all their efforts are in vain. St Thomas More's Anthony suggests that the alternative to the behaviour of the 'burdenouse & hevy comfortours' is to tell an afflicted person 'to stand & percever still in the confession of his faith', so that 'all his hole payne shall tourne all into glorye' (*Dialogue of Comfort*, 1.10).

Burton, in his *Anatomy of Melancholy* (3.4.1.1), compares the comforters to the 'Schismaticks' and 'Hereticks' of his day: 'they speak not, they think not, they write not well of God, and as they ought.' Shakespeare's allusion to the comforters in *Othello* 4.2.48–57 is indirect. Othello suggests that his lot is harder than Job's. He could bear becoming 'the fixed figure for the time of scorn / To point his slow unmoving finger at!' – but he could not bear Desdemona's faithlessness. Sir Thomas Browne echoes Calvin's verdict when he calls the 'oblique expostulations' of Job's friends 'a deeper injury than the downe-right blows of the Devill' (*Religio Medici*, 2.5; cf. *Pseudodoxia Epidemica*, 7.8).

Dryden speculates on the comforters' later actions: 'The friends of Job, who rail'd at him before, / Came cap in hand when he had three times more' ('Prologue to His Royal Highness', 24–25). One of the few positive evaluations of their behaviour occurs at the beginning of Defoe's *Roxana*. The heroine, left by her husband and facing destitution, is visited by two women: 'They sat down like *Job's* three Comforters, and said not one Word to me for a great while, but both of them cry'd as fast, and as heartily as I did.' Swift's allusion (in *Ingenious Conversation*, 3) is disparaging, as is Fielding's in *Tom Jones*. Tom receives a letter from Sophia that asks him not to visit her again: 'This Letter administered the same Kind of Consolation to poor *Jones*, which *Job* formerly received from his Friends' (14.3).

Cowper, in his poem 'Retirement', characterizes Job's comforters and those of his own time as

> Blest, rather curst, with hearts that never feel,
> Kept snug in caskets of close-hammer'd steel,
> With mouths made only to grin wide and eat,
> And minds that deem derided pain a treat. (307–10)

In a curiously mistaken reference, Byron's *Don Juan* mentions Job's 'two friends'. The misanthropic lesson Byron offers is that they are 'but bad pilots when the weather's rough' (14.48). Blake's *Illustrations of the Book of Job* depicts the development of genuinely sympathetic friends into accusers.

A man named Bildad is half-owner of Captain Ahab's ship *Pequod* in Melville's *Moby Dick*. As N. Wright (1949) has observed, 'He seems to practice piety and to aim at the conversion of all his sailors in order to insure a prosperous voyage for the *Pequod*.' The ironic depiction of his pragmatism recalls the utilitarianism of his biblical counterpart (cf. Melville's comparison of the ambiguous characters Old Plain Talk and Old Prudence to Eliphaz and Bildad in China Aster's story, chapter 40 of *The Confidence-Man*). The economic implications of the friends' speeches are also recognized by John Ruskin. In his introduction to *The Bible of Amiens*, he calls Zophar's second speech the 'leading piece of political economy'.

In Anthony Trollope's *Barchester Towers* (2.17), Mary Bold is praised for not being triumphant when her sister-in-law describes her involvement in all the intrigues she had already been warned against: '"I told you so, I told you so!" is the croak of a true Job's comforter. But Mary, when she found her friend lying in her sorrow and scraping herself with potsherds, forbore to argue and to exult.' Fulkerson, in W. D. Howells' *A Hazard of New Fortunes*, feels he is not treated so kindly. He reacts to the irony of Beaton by saying: 'Go on, Bildad. Like to sprinkle a few ashes over my boils?' (4.9). Hardy's poem 'In the Seventies' has as a motto the Vulgate version of Job 12:4: *'Qui deridetur ab amico suo sicut ego.'* The poem thus identifies as Job's comforters those friends of the poet's who did not take his literary ambitions seriously.

Frost's Job, in *A Masque of Reason*, contemptuously calls his comforters 'that committee'; God continues in a jocular tone:

I saw you had no fondness for committees.
Next time you find yourself pressed onto one
For the revision of the Book of Prayer
Put that in if it isn't in already:
Deliver us from committees. 'Twill remind me. (368–73)

Equally humorous is the reference to Bildad in a riddle in Carl Sandburg's *The People, Yes* (46): his cognomen 'Shuhite' ('shoe-height') marks him as one of the shortest people in the Bible.

Samuel Beckett compares the appearance of his character Murphy, who is 'on the jobpath' (an obvious pun), to Blake's picture of Bildad. The narrator remarks that Bildad is 'but a fragment of Job, as Zophar and the others are fragments of Job. The only thing Murphy was seeking was what he had not ceased to seek from the moment of his being strangled into a state of respiration – the best of himself' (*Murphy*, chapter 5). If such psychologizing reflects 20th-century thinking, Archibald MacLeish's *J.B.* may be said to do so even more systematically. It attempts to show how the role of modern comforters differs from that of the biblical ones: 'Where Job's comforters undertook to persuade him, against the evidence of his own inner conviction, that he WAS guilty, ours attempts to persuade us that we are not...' (MacLeish). *J.B.*'s Eliphaz is a modern scientist (he wears an intern's jacket) who tries to explain guilt away as an illusion. Bildad, in turn, a leftist park-bench orator, calls it a 'sociological accident'; and Zophar, who wears 'the wreck of a clerical collar' and seems to represent theology, puts the blame for mankind's sin on the Creator. All three fail to understand the Distant Voice of God when it speaks to J.B.

Harvey Gotham, the stricken hero of Muriel Spark's *The Only Problem*, considers the comforters 'very patient and considerate' in their trying to relieve Job's suffering: they keep him talking like an analyst's patient on the couch (chapter 3). On the other hand, Gotham sees the Job narrative as teaching 'the futility of friendship in times of trouble. That is perhaps not a reflection on friends but on friendship. Friends mean well, or make as if they do. But friendship itself is made for happiness, not trouble' (chapter 9).

Manfred Siebald
Johannes Gutenberg Universität, Mainz, Germany

Morning Stars Sang Together

To Job's questioning of God's justice, the Lord replies out of the whirlwind in a series of his own questions, revealing the utter inadequacy of Job's perspective: 'Where wast thou when I laid the foundations of the earth?... When the morning stars sang together, and all the sons of God shouted for joy?' (Job 38:4, 7).

Carlyle's Professor Teufelsdröckh, who seems not to have recollected Job's humbling, writes, 'Is not Man's History, and Men's History, a perpetual Evangel? Listen, and for organ-music thou wilt ever, as of old, hear the Morning Stars sing together' (*Sartor Resartus*, 3.7). For Whittier, in 'The Worship of Nature', the song likewise continues:

> The harp at Nature's advent strung
> Has never ceased to play;
> The song the stars of morning sang
> Has never died away.

In D.G. Rossetti's *The Blessed Damozel*, the allusion is somewhat better contextualized:

> Her gaze still strove
> Within the gulf to pierce
> Its path; and now she spoke as when
> The stars sang in their spheres.

David L. Jeffrey
University of Ottawa

Naked Came I

This phrase was uttered by Job in his first statement of acceptance of the great calamities which had fallen upon his household: 'Naked came I out of my mother's womb, and naked shall I return thither: the Lord gave, and the Lord hath taken away; blessed be the name of the Lord' (1:21). These words are typically coupled in Christian commentary with St Paul's reminder that 'We brought nothing into the world, and it is certain we can carry nothing out' (1 Timothy 6:7; cf. St Jerome, *Epistle* 22.32). Among the Fathers of the Church the passage is consistently applied to an understanding of the problems of death and suffering; even in the midst of trouble one should not lose faith in the persistent goodness of God. In a letter of support for a widow, directed to her friend Marcello, Jerome writes,

> God is good, and all that he does must be good also. Does he decree that I must lose my husband? I mourn my loss, but because it is his will I bear it with resignation. Is an only son snatched from me? The blow is hard, yet it can be borne, for He who has taken away is He who gave. (*Epistle* 39.2; cf. *Epistle* 127.13–14)

Matthew Henry (*Commentary* 3.11–12) follows Calvin in observing the similarity of Job's and Paul's formulations to parallel statements in Seneca and Epictetus.

The normative application of the text leads in both Jewish and Christian tradition to its invocation in funeral litany and oration. The passage has also been connected (with reference to the image of the womb) to Nicodemus' question to Jesus: 'How can a man be born when he is old? Can he enter the second time into his mother's womb, and be born?' (John 3:4).

Chaucer's patient Griselda, tested extravagantly by her husband, the marquis Walter, is at last sent by him back to her humble place of origin stripped of her royal clothing and wedding ring. She replies (*Clerk's Tale*, 4.865–72) with exemplary Christian resignation:

> 'To yow broughte I nought elles, out of drede,
> But feith, and nakednesse, and maydenhede...
> Naked out of my fadres hous', quod she,
> 'I cam, and naked moot I turne agayn.'

In Oliver Goldsmith's *The Vicar of Wakefield* the unfortunate and Job-like vicar, enraged over his daughter's seduction, is admonished by his son for cursing her kidnapper. Recomposing himself, he reflects that a 'more than human benevolence has taught us to bless our enemies: Blessed be His holy name for all the good He hath given, and for all that He hath taken away' (chapter 17; cf. Matthew 5:44). In the

Victorian *Framley Parsonage* by Anthony Trollope, the verse is more dubiously applied in an expression of gratitude or relief that calamity has fallen upon neighbours but spared the parsonage (chapter 48).

David L. Jeffrey
University of Ottawa

Satan *see* Devil (Satan)

Though He Slay Me

In the first round of the conversations in which Job's friends Eliphaz, Bildad, and Zophar try to convince him that he deserves the calamities which have befallen him, Zophar speaks last (Job 11). He points out Job's limitations, God's infinity, and the necessity of repentance. In his reply (chapters 12–14), Job surpasses Zophar in the depiction of God's grandeur and accuses his friends of presumptuous talk. His desire 'to reason with God' (13:2) is so overwhelming that he claims, 'Though he slay me, yet will I trust in him: but I will maintain mine own ways before him' (13:15). The rest of Job's speech is a direct address to God.

The Hebrew text of Job 13:15 poses several problems which have led to largely divergent translations. The King James Version follows the Geneva, which in turn agrees with the Vulgate in giving the main clause a positive meaning. The Revised Standard Version, however, translates, 'Behold, he will slay me; I have no hope. Yet I will defend my ways to his face.' Whether one rejects the King James Version wording as a 'sublime mistranslation' (*Interpreter's Bible*) or argues for its appropriateness, it has had by far the greatest influence on English literature.

For St Gregory the Great (*Moralia in Iob*) the verse is a reminder that the virtue of patience is seldom found in the midst of prosperity: 'Hereby the righteous mind is distinguished from the unrighteous – that even in the midst of adversity the former offers praise to omnipotent God.' St Bonaventure similarly stresses Job's expression of patience and confidence in God (*Expositio in Psalterium*, 119.109).

According to Calvin, the passage indicates that God 'lets the believers fall in order to test and improve their faith'. Moreover, death is 'like a blunt sword', which cannot injure us (*Sermons on Job*). John Donne, preaching on this text, tries to solve the textual problem by reading, 'Behold he will kill me, yet shall not I hope in him?' and goes on to assert that God's omnipotence can indeed mean destruction to humanity. Yet 'though he end a weary life, with a painefull death, as there is no other hope, but in him, so there needs no other, for that alone is both abundant, and infallible in its selfe.' In Thomas Hooker's words, the verse reads, 'Thou makest me a butt to shoot at; yet I will trust in thee though thou kill me' – which for him illustrates the fact that 'A man's faith may be somewhat strong when his feeling is nothing at all' ('The Poor Doubting Christian'). For John Henry Newman, in his sermon on 'Peace and Joy Amid Chastisement', Job's words reflect 'that state of mingled hope and fear, of peace and anxiety, of grace and insecurity' which people are in because 'the sins which we commit here… are not put away absolutely and once for all, but are in one sense upon us till the Judgment.' Burton places Job in the ranks of the martyrs who endured with patience and willingness 'the utmost that human rage and fury could invent' (*Anatomy of Melancholy*, 2.3.3).

Carlyle secularizes the sentence and gives it an ironic twist when he complains about being the 'doomed everlasting prey of the Quack' in his essay 'The Gospel of Mammonism' (*Past and Present*, 3.2). He concludes, 'Though he slay me, yet will I *not* trust in him.' In a similar vein, Melville uses the verse as a motto for his poem 'The Enthusiast', which depicts an attitude of defiance against life's adversities and against bourgeois superficiality.

Miss Jessie Brown in Elizabeth Gaskell's *Cranford* repeats Job's words as a statement of trust in God after the loss of her father and while her only sister is dying (chapter 2). In 'Later Life', Christina Rossetti first paraphrases the verse and then gives it an eschatological twist: 'Yea, though He slay us we will vaunt his praise, / Serving and loving with the cherubim…' In Whittier's 'Barclay of Ury', Barclay expresses his spiritual resignation: 'Passive to his holy will, / Trust I in my Master still, / Even though he slay me.' Less resigned but echoing Job's words is Emily Dickinson's poem 'Bind me – I still can sing'.

In his preface to *St Joan*, George Bernard Shaw puts special emphasis on the second part of the verse ('but I will maintain my own ways before him') to characterize his Joan. American novelist Theodore Dreiser uses Job's words to describe the Quakers' traditional attitude towards God (*The Bulwark*, 'Introduction'). In Archibald MacLeish's Job drama, J.B. accentuates the difference between the first and the second parts of the statement by uttering the first part 'violently' and, after some silence, the second part with dropped voice (*J.B.*, 9). Yakov Bok's father-in-law Shmuel, in Bernard Malamud's novel *The Fixer*, tries to convince the unjustly imprisoned Yakov of God's justice and the necessity to trust in him: 'He invented light, He created the world. He made us both. The true miracle is belief. I believe in Him. Job said, "Though he slay me, yet will I trust in Him."' Freethinking Yakov, however, dismisses Job as an invention. In Malamud's *God's Grace*, God repeatedly announces that he will have to 'slay' protagonist Calvin Cohn. Even though Cohn's death is postponed, he does not, however, trust in God.

Manfred Siebald
Johannes Gutenberg Universität, Mainz, Germany

THE BOOK OF JOB

Prologue

Satan's Challenge

Job 1:1 – 3:26

There was a man in the land of Uz, whose name was Job; and that man was perfect and upright, and one that feared God, and eschewed evil. And there were born unto him seven sons and three daughters. His substance also was seven thousand sheep, and three thousand camels, and five hundred yoke of oxen, and five hundred she asses, and a very great household; so that this man was the greatest of all the men of the east.

And his sons went and feasted in their houses, every one his day; and sent and called for their three sisters to eat and to drink with them. And it was so, when the days of their feasting were gone about, that Job sent and sanctified them, and rose up early in the morning, and offered burnt offerings according to the number of them all: for Job said, It may be that my sons have sinned, and cursed God in their hearts. Thus did Job continually.

Now there was a day when the sons of God came to present themselves before the Lord, and Satan came also among them. And the Lord said unto Satan, Whence comest thou?

Then Satan answered the Lord, and said, From going to and fro in the earth, and from walking up and down in it.

And the Lord said unto Satan, Hast thou considered my servant Job, that there is none like him in the earth, a perfect and an upright man, one that feareth God, and escheweth evil?

Then Satan answered the Lord, and said, Doth Job fear God for nought? Hast not thou made an hedge about him, and about his house, and about all that he hath on every side? thou hast blessed the work of his hands, and his substance is increased in the land. But put forth thine hand now, and touch all that he hath, and he will curse thee to thy face.

And the Lord said unto Satan, Behold, all that he hath is in thy power; only upon himself put not forth thine hand.

So Satan went forth from the presence of the Lord.

And there was a day when his sons and his daughters were eating and drinking wine in their eldest brother's house: And there came a messenger unto Job, and said, The oxen were plowing, and the asses feeding beside them: And the Sabeans fell upon them, and took them away; yea, they have slain the servants with the edge of the sword; and I only am escaped alone to tell thee.

While he was yet speaking, there came also another, and said, The fire of God is fallen from heaven, and hath burned up the sheep, and the servants, and consumed them; and I only am escaped alone to tell thee.

While he was yet speaking, there came also another, and said, The Chaldeans made out three bands, and fell upon the camels, and have carried them away, yea, and slain the servants with the edge of the sword; and I only am escaped alone to tell thee.

While he was yet speaking, there came also another, and said, Thy sons and thy daughters were eating and drinking wine in their eldest brother's house: And, behold, there came a great wind from the wilderness, and smote the four corners of the house, and it fell upon the young men, and they are dead; and I only am escaped alone to tell thee.

Then Job arose, and rent his mantle, and shaved his head, and fell down upon the ground, and worshipped, And said,

> Naked came I out of my mother's womb,
>   and naked shall I return thither:
> the Lord gave, and the Lord hath taken away;
>   blessed be the name of the Lord.

In all this Job sinned not, nor charged God foolishly.

Again there was a day when the sons of God came to present themselves before the Lord, and Satan came also among them to present himself before the Lord.

And the Lord said unto Satan, From whence comest thou? And Satan answered the Lord, and said, From going to and fro in the earth, and from walking up and down in it.

And the Lord said unto Satan, Hast thou considered my servant Job, that there is none like him in the earth, a perfect and an upright man, one that feareth God, and escheweth evil? and still he holdeth fast his integrity, although thou movedst me against him, to destroy him without cause.

And Satan answered the Lord, and said, Skin for skin, yea, all that a man hath will he give for his life. But put forth thine hand now, and touch his bone and his flesh, and he will curse thee to thy face.

And the Lord said unto Satan, Behold, he is in thine hand; but save his life.

So went Satan forth from the presence of the Lord, and smote Job with sore boils from the sole of his foot unto his crown. And he took him a potsherd to scrape himself withal; and he sat down among the ashes.

Then said his wife unto him, Dost thou still retain thine integrity? curse God, and die.

But he said unto her, Thou speakest as one of the foolish women speaketh. What? shall we receive good at the hand of God, and shall we not receive evil?

In all this did not Job sin with his lips.

Now when Job's three friends heard of all this evil that was come upon him, they came every one from his own place; Eliphaz the Temanite, and Bildad the Shuhite, and Zophar the Naamathite: for they had made an appointment together to come to mourn with him and to comfort him. And when they lifted up their eyes afar off, and knew him not, they lifted up their voice, and wept; and they rent every one his mantle, and sprinkled dust upon their heads toward heaven. So they sat down with him upon the ground seven days and seven nights, and none spake a word unto him: for they saw that his grief was very great.

After this opened Job his mouth, and cursed his day. And Job spake, and said,

> Let the day perish wherein I was born,
>> and the night in which it was said,
>>> There is a man child conceived.
> Let that day be darkness;
>> let not God regard it from above,
>> neither let the light shine upon it.

Let darkness and the shadow of death stain it;
>   let a cloud dwell upon it;
>   let the blackness of the day terrify it.
As for that night, let darkness seize upon it;
>   let it not be joined unto the days of the year,
>   let it not come into the number of the months.
Lo, let that night be solitary,
>   let no joyful voice come therein.
Let them curse it that curse the day,
>   who are ready to raise up their mourning.
Let the stars of the twilight thereof be dark;
>   let it look for light, but have none;
>   neither let it see the dawning of the day:
Because it shut not up the doors of my mother's womb,
>   nor hid sorrow from mine eyes.

Why died I not from the womb?
>   why did I not give up the ghost when I came out of
>   the belly?
Why did the knees prevent me?
>   or why the breasts that I should suck?
For now should I have lain still and been quiet,
>   I should have slept: then had I been at rest,
With kings and counsellors of the earth,
>   which build desolate places for themselves;
Or with princes that had gold,
>   who filled their houses with silver:
Or as an hidden untimely birth I had not been;
>   as infants which never saw light.
There the wicked cease from troubling;
>   and there the weary be at rest.
There the prisoners rest together;
>   they hear not the voice of the oppressor.
The small and great are there;
>   and the servant is free from his master.

Wherefore is light given to him that is in misery,
>   and life unto the bitter in soul;

Which long for death, but it cometh not;
    and dig for it more than for hid treasures;
Which rejoice exceedingly,
    and are glad, when they can find the grave?
Why is light given to a man
    whose way is hid,
    and whom God hath hedged in?
For my sighing cometh before I eat,
    and my roarings are poured out like the waters.
For the thing which I greatly feared is come upon me,
    and that which I was afraid of is come unto me.
I was not in safety, neither had I rest,
    neither was I quiet; yet trouble came.

Part One

The First Cycle of Speeches

Job 4:1 – 14:22

Eliphaz

Then Eliphaz the Temanite answered and said,

If we assay to commune with thee, wilt thou be grieved?
 but who can withhold himself from speaking?
Behold, thou hast instructed many,
 and thou hast strengthened the weak hands.
Thy words have upholden him that was falling,
 and thou hast strengthened the feeble knees.
But now it is come upon thee, and thou faintest;
 it toucheth thee, and thou art troubled.
Is not this thy fear, thy confidence,
 thy hope, and the uprightness of thy ways?

Remember, I pray thee, who ever perished, being innocent?
 or where were the righteous cut off?
Even as I have seen, they that plow iniquity,
 and sow wickedness, reap the same.
By the blast of God they perish,
 and by the breath of his nostrils are they consumed.
The roaring of the lion, and the voice of the fierce lion,
 and the teeth of the young lions, are broken.
The old lion perisheth for lack of prey,
 and the stout lion's whelps are scattered abroad.

Now a thing was secretly brought to me,
 and mine ear received a little thereof.
In thoughts from the visions of the night,
 when deep sleep falleth on men,

Fear came upon me, and trembling,
    which made all my bones to shake.
Then a spirit passed before my face;
    the hair of my flesh stood up:
It stood still,
    but I could not discern the form thereof:
an image was before mine eyes, there was silence,
    and I heard a voice, saying,
Shall mortal man be more just than God?
    shall a man be more pure than his maker?
Behold, he put no trust in his servants;
    and his angels he charged with folly:
How much less in them that dwell in houses of clay,
    whose foundation is in the dust,
    which are crushed before the moth?
They are destroyed from morning to evening:
    they perish for ever without any regarding it.
Doth not their excellency which is in them go away?
    they die, even without wisdom.

Call now, if there be any that will answer thee;
    and to which of the saints wilt thou turn?
For wrath killeth the foolish man,
    and envy slayeth the silly one.
I have seen the foolish taking root:
    but suddenly I cursed his habitation.
His children are far from safety,
    and they are crushed in the gate,
    neither is there any to deliver them.
Whose harvest the hungry eateth up,
    and taketh it even out of the thorns,
    and the robber swalloweth up their substance.
Although affliction cometh not forth of the dust,
    neither doth trouble spring out of the ground;
Yet man is born unto trouble,
    as the sparks fly upward.

I would seek unto God,
    and unto God would I commit my cause:

Which doeth great things and unsearchable;
    marvellous things without number:
Who giveth rain upon the earth,
    and sendeth waters upon the fields:
To set up on high those that be low;
    that those which mourn may be exalted to safety.
He disappointeth the devices of the crafty,
    so that their hands cannot perform their enterprise.
He taketh the wise in their own craftiness:
    and the counsel of the froward is carried headlong.
They meet with darkness in the daytime,
    and grope in the noonday as in the night.
But he saveth the poor from the sword, from their mouth,
    and from the hand of the mighty.
So the poor hath hope, and iniquity stoppeth her mouth.

Behold, happy is the man whom God correcteth:
    therefore despise not thou the chastening of the Almighty:
For he maketh sore, and bindeth up:
    he woundeth, and his hands make whole.
He shall deliver thee in six troubles:
    yea, in seven there shall no evil touch thee.
In famine he shall redeem thee from death:
    and in war from the power of the sword.
Thou shalt be hid from the scourge of the tongue:
    neither shalt thou be afraid of destruction when it cometh.
At destruction and famine thou shalt laugh:
    neither shalt thou be afraid of the beasts of the earth.
For thou shalt be in league with the stones of the field:
    and the beasts of the field shall be at peace with thee.
And thou shalt know that thy tabernacle shall be in peace;
    and thou shalt visit thy habitation, and shalt not sin.
Thou shalt know also that thy seed shall be great,
    and thine offspring as the grass of the earth.
Thou shalt come to thy grave in a full age,
    like as a shock of corn cometh in in his season.

Lo this, we have searched it, so it is;
    hear it, and know thou it for thy good.

Job

But Job answered and said,

> Oh that my grief were throughly weighed,
>> and my calamity laid in the balances together!
> For now it would be heavier than the sand of the sea:
>> therefore my words are swallowed up.
> For the arrows of the Almighty are within me,
>> the poison whereof drinketh up my spirit:
>> the terrors of God do set themselves in array against me.
> Doth the wild ass bray when he hath grass?
>> or loweth the ox over his fodder?
> Can that which is unsavoury be eaten without salt?
>> or is there any taste in the white of an egg?
> The things that my soul refused to touch
>> are as my sorrowful meat.

> Oh that I might have my request;
>> and that God would grant me the thing that I long for!
> Even that it would please God to destroy me;
>> that he would let loose his hand, and cut me off!
> Then should I yet have comfort; yea, I would harden myself
>>> in sorrow:
>> let him not spare;
>> for I have not concealed the words of the Holy One.

> What is my strength, that I should hope?
>> and what is mine end, that I should prolong my life?
> Is my strength the strength of stones?
>> or is my flesh of brass?
> Is not my help in me?
>> and is wisdom driven quite from me?

> To him that is afflicted pity should be shewed from his friend;
>> but he forsaketh the fear of the Almighty.
> My brethren have dealt deceitfully as a brook,
>> and as the stream of brooks they pass away;

Which are blackish by reason of the ice,
    and wherein the snow is hid:
What time they wax warm, they vanish:
    when it is hot, they are consumed out of their place.
The paths of their way are turned aside;
    they go to nothing, and perish.
The troops of Tema looked,
    the companies of Sheba waited for them.
They were confounded because they had hoped;
    they came thither, and were ashamed.
For now ye are nothing;
    ye see my casting down, and are afraid.
Did I say, Bring unto me?
    or, Give a reward for me of your substance?
Or, Deliver me from the enemy's hand?
    or, Redeem me from the hand of the mighty?

Teach me, and I will hold my tongue:
    and cause me to understand wherein I have erred.
How forcible are right words!
    but what doth your arguing reprove?
Do ye imagine to reprove words,
    and the speeches of one that is desperate, which are
      as wind?
Yea, ye overwhelm the fatherless,
    and ye dig a pit for your friend.
Now therefore be content, look upon me;
    for it is evident unto you if I lie.
Return, I pray you, let it not be iniquity;
    yea, return again, my righteousness is in it.
Is there iniquity in my tongue?
    cannot my taste discern perverse things?

Is there not an appointed time to man upon earth?
    are not his days also like the days of an hireling?
As a servant earnestly desireth the shadow,
    and as an hireling looketh for the reward of his work:

So am I made to possess months of vanity,
    and wearisome nights are appointed to me.
When I lie down, I say, When shall I arise, and the night
      be gone?
    and I am full of tossings to and fro unto the dawning of
        the day.
My flesh is clothed with worms and clods of dust;
    my skin is broken, and become loathsome.

My days are swifter than a weaver's shuttle,
    and are spent without hope.
O remember that my life is wind:
    mine eye shall no more see good.
The eye of him that hath seen me shall see me no more:
    thine eyes are upon me, and I am not.
As the cloud is consumed and vanisheth away:
    so he that goeth down to the grave shall come up no more.
He shall return no more to his house,
    neither shall his place know him any more.

Therefore I will not refrain my mouth;
    I will speak in the anguish of my spirit;
    I will complain in the bitterness of my soul.
Am I a sea, or a whale,
    that thou settest a watch over me?
When I say, My bed shall comfort me,
    my couch shall ease my complaints;
Then thou scarest me with dreams,
    and terrifiest me through visions:
So that my soul chooseth strangling,
    and death rather than my life.
I loathe it; I would not live alway:
    let me alone; for my days are vanity.

What is man, that thou shouldest magnify him?
    and that thou shouldest set thine heart upon him?
And that thou shouldest visit him every morning,
    and try him every moment?

How long wilt thou not depart from me,
    nor let me alone till I swallow down my spittle?
I have sinned; what shall I do unto thee,
    O thou preserver of men?
why hast thou set me as a mark against thee,
    so that I am a burden to myself?
And why dost thou not pardon my transgression,
    and take away my iniquity?
for now shall I sleep in the dust;
    and thou shalt seek me in the morning, but I shall not be.

Bildad

Then answered Bildad the Shuhite, and said,

How long wilt thou speak these things?
    and how long shall the words of thy mouth be like a
        strong wind?
Doth God pervert judgment?
    or doth the Almighty pervert justice?
If thy children have sinned against him,
    and he have cast them away for their transgression;
If thou wouldest seek unto God betimes,
    and make thy supplication to the Almighty;
If thou wert pure and upright;
    surely now he would awake for thee,
    and make the habitation of thy righteousness prosperous.
Though thy beginning was small,
    yet thy latter end should greatly increase.

For enquire, I pray thee, of the former age,
    and prepare thyself to the search of their fathers:
(For we are but of yesterday, and know nothing,
    because our days upon earth are a shadow:)
Shall not they teach thee, and tell thee,
    and utter words out of their heart?

Can the rush grow up without mire?
　　can the flag grow without water?
Whilst it is yet in his greenness, and not cut down,
　　it withereth before any other herb.
So are the paths of all that forget God;
　　and the hypocrite's hope shall perish:
Whose hope shall be cut off,
　　and whose trust shall be a spider's web.
He shall lean upon his house, but it shall not stand:
　　he shall hold it fast, but it shall not endure.
He is green before the sun,
　　and his branch shooteth forth in his garden.
His roots are wrapped about the heap,
　　and seeth the place of stones.
If he destroy him from his place,
　　then it shall deny him, saying, I have not seen thee.
Behold, this is the joy of his way,
　　and out of the earth shall others grow.

Behold, God will not cast away a perfect man,
　　neither will he help the evil doers:
Till he fill thy mouth with laughing,
　　and thy lips with rejoicing.
They that hate thee shall be clothed with shame;
　　and the dwelling place of the wicked shall come to nought.

Job

Then Job answered and said,

　　I know it is so of a truth:
　　　　but how should man be just with God?
　　If he will contend with him,
　　　　he cannot answer him one of a thousand.
　　He is wise in heart, and mighty in strength:
　　　　who hath hardened himself against him, and hath prospered?
　　Which removeth the mountains, and they know not:
　　　　which overturneth them in his anger.

Which shaketh the earth out of her place,
    and the pillars thereof tremble.
Which commandeth the sun, and it riseth not;
    and sealeth up the stars.
Which alone spreadeth out the heavens,
    and treadeth upon the waves of the sea.
Which maketh Arcturus, Orion, and Pleiades,
    and the chambers of the south.
Which doeth great things past finding out;
    yea, and wonders without number.
Lo, he goeth by me, and I see him not:
    he passeth on also, but I perceive him not.
Behold, he taketh away, who can hinder him?
    who will say unto him, What doest thou?
If God will not withdraw his anger,
    the proud helpers do stoop under him.

How much less shall I answer him,
    and choose out my words to reason with him?
Whom, though I were righteous, yet would I not answer,
    but I would make supplication to my judge.
If I had called, and he had answered me;
    yet would I not believe that he had hearkened unto my voice.
For he breaketh me with a tempest,
    and multiplieth my wounds without cause.
He will not suffer me to take my breath,
    but filleth me with bitterness.
If I speak of strength, lo, he is strong:
    and if of judgment, who shall set me a time to plead?
If I justify myself, mine own mouth shall condemn me:
    if I say, I am perfect, it shall also prove me perverse.

Though I were perfect,
    yet would I not know my soul:
    I would despise my life.
This is one thing, therefore I said it,
    He destroyeth the perfect and the wicked.

If the scourge slay suddenly,
    he will laugh at the trial of the innocent.
The earth is given into the hand of the wicked:
    he covereth the faces of the judges thereof;
    if not, where, and who is he?

Now my days are swifter than a post:
    they flee away, they see no good.
They are passed away as the swift ships:
    as the eagle that hasteth to the prey.
If I say, I will forget my complaint,
    I will leave off my heaviness, and comfort myself:
I am afraid of all my sorrows,
    I know that thou wilt not hold me innocent.
If I be wicked,
    why then labour I in vain?
If I wash myself with snow water,
    and make my hands never so clean;
Yet shalt thou plunge me in the ditch,
    and mine own clothes shall abhor me.

For he is not a man, as I am, that I should answer him,
    and we should come together in judgment.
Neither is there any daysman betwixt us,
    that might lay his hand upon us both.
Let him take his rod away from me,
    and let not his fear terrify me:
Then would I speak, and not fear him;
    but it is not so with me.

My soul is weary of my life;
    I will leave my complaint upon myself;
    I will speak in the bitterness of my soul.
I will say unto God, Do not condemn me;
    shew me wherefore thou contendest with me.
Is it good unto thee that thou shouldest oppress,
    that thou shouldest despise the work of thine hands,
    and shine upon the counsel of the wicked?

Hast thou eyes of flesh?
  or seest thou as man seeth?
Are thy days as the days of man?
  are thy years as man's days,
That thou enquirest after mine iniquity,
  and searchest after my sin?
Thou knowest that I am not wicked;
  and there is none that can deliver out of thine hand.

Thine hands have made me and fashioned me together
    round about;
  yet thou dost destroy me.
Remember, I beseech thee, that thou hast made me as the clay;
  and wilt thou bring me into dust again?
Hast thou not poured me out as milk,
  and curdled me like cheese?
Thou hast clothed me with skin and flesh,
  and hast fenced me with bones and sinews.
Thou hast granted me life and favour,
  and thy visitation hath preserved my spirit.

And these things hast thou hid in thine heart:
  I know that this is with thee.
If I sin, then thou markest me,
  and thou wilt not acquit me from mine iniquity.
If I be wicked, woe unto me;
  and if I be righteous, yet will I not lift up my head.
I am full of confusion;
  therefore see thou mine affliction;
For it increaseth. Thou huntest me as a fierce lion:
  and again thou shewest thyself marvellous upon me.
Thou renewest thy witnesses against me,
  and increasest thine indignation upon me;
  changes and war are against me.

Wherefore then hast thou brought me forth out of the womb?
  Oh that I had given up the ghost, and no eye had seen me!

I should have been as though I had not been;
  I should have been carried from the womb to the grave.
Are not my days few?
  cease then, and let me alone, that I may take comfort a little,
Before I go whence I shall not return,
  even to the land of darkness and the shadow of death;
A land of darkness, as darkness itself;
  and of the shadow of death, without any order,
  and where the light is as darkness.

Zophar

Then answered Zophar the Naamathite, and said,

Should not the multitude of words be answered?
  and should a man full of talk be justified?
Should thy lies make men hold their peace?
  and when thou mockest, shall no man make thee ashamed?
For thou hast said, My doctrine is pure,
  and I am clean in thine eyes.
But oh that God would speak,
  and open his lips against thee;
And that he would shew thee the secrets of wisdom,
  that they are double to that which is!
Know therefore that God exacteth of thee less than thine
  iniquity deserveth.

Canst thou by searching find out God?
  canst thou find out the Almighty unto perfection?
It is as high as heaven; what canst thou do?
  deeper than hell; what canst thou know?
The measure thereof is longer than the earth,
  and broader than the sea.

If he cut off, and shut up,
  or gather together, then who can hinder him?
For he knoweth vain men:
  he seeth wickedness also; will he not then consider it?

For vain men would be wise,
    though man be born like a wild ass' colt.

If thou prepare thine heart,
    and stretch out thine hands toward him;
If iniquity be in thine hand, put it far away,
    and let not wickedness dwell in thy tabernacles.
For then shalt thou lift up thy face without spot;
    yea, thou shalt be stedfast, and shalt not fear:
Because thou shalt forget thy misery,
    and remember it as waters that pass away:
And thine age shall be clearer than the noonday;
    thou shalt shine forth, thou shalt be as the morning.
And thou shalt be secure, because there is hope;
    yea, thou shalt dig about thee, and thou shalt take thy
        rest in safety.
Also thou shalt lie down, and none shall make thee afraid;
    yea, many shall make suit unto thee.
But the eyes of the wicked shall fail,
    and they shall not escape,
    and their hope shall be as the giving up of the ghost.

Job

And Job answered and said,

No doubt but ye are the people,
    and wisdom shall die with you.
But I have understanding as well as you;
    I am not inferior to you:
    yea, who knoweth not such things as these?

I am as one mocked of his neighbour,
    who calleth upon God, and he answereth him:
    the just upright man is laughed to scorn.
He that is ready to slip with his feet is as a lamp despised
    in the thought of him that is at ease.

The tabernacles of robbers prosper,
    and they that provoke God are secure;
    into whose hand God bringeth abundantly.

But ask now the beasts, and they shall teach thee;
    and the fowls of the air, and they shall tell thee:
Or speak to the earth, and it shall teach thee:
    and the fishes of the sea shall declare unto thee.
Who knoweth not in all these
    that the hand of the Lord hath wrought this?
In whose hand is the soul of every living thing,
    and the breath of all mankind.
Doth not the ear try words?
    and the mouth taste his meat?
With the ancient is wisdom;
    and in length of days understanding.
With him is wisdom and strength,
    he hath counsel and understanding.
Behold, he breaketh down, and it cannot be built again:
    he shutteth up a man, and there can be no opening.
Behold, he withholdeth the waters, and they dry up:
    also he sendeth them out, and they overturn the earth.
With him is strength and wisdom:
    the deceived and the deceiver are his.
He leadeth counsellors away spoiled,
    and maketh the judges fools.
He looseth the bond of kings,
    and girdeth their loins with a girdle.
He leadeth princes away spoiled,
    and overthroweth the mighty.
He removeth away the speech of the trusty,
    and taketh away the understanding of the aged.
He poureth contempt upon princes,
    and weakeneth the strength of the mighty.
He discovereth deep things out of darkness,
    and bringeth out to light the shadow of death.

He increaseth the nations, and destroyeth them:
  he enlargeth the nations, and straiteneth them again.
He taketh away the heart of the chief of the people of the earth,
  and causeth them to wander in a wilderness where there
    is no way.
They grope in the dark without light,
  and he maketh them to stagger like a drunken man.

Lo, mine eye hath seen all this,
  mine ear hath heard and understood it.
What ye know, the same do I know also:
  I am not inferior unto you.
Surely I would speak to the Almighty,
  and I desire to reason with God.
But ye are forgers of lies,
  ye are all physicians of no value.
O that ye would altogether hold your peace!
  and it should be your wisdom.
Hear now my reasoning,
  and hearken to the pleadings of my lips.
Will ye speak wickedly for God?
  and talk deceitfully for him?
Will ye accept his person?
  will ye contend for God?
Is it good that he should search you out?
  or as one man mocketh another, do ye so mock him?
He will surely reprove you,
  if ye do secretly accept persons.
Shall not his excellency make you afraid?
  and his dread fall upon you?
Your remembrances are like unto ashes,
  your bodies to bodies of clay.

Hold your peace, let me alone, that I may speak,
  and let come on me what will.
Wherefore do I take my flesh in my teeth,
  and put my life in mine hand?

Though he slay me, yet will I trust in him:
  but I will maintain mine own ways before him.
He also shall be my salvation:
  for an hypocrite shall not come before him.
Hear diligently my speech,
  and my declaration with your ears.
Behold now, I have ordered my cause;
  I know that I shall be justified.
Who is he that will plead with me?
  for now, if I hold my tongue, I shall give up the ghost.

Only do not two things unto me:
  then will I not hide myself from thee.
Withdraw thine hand far from me:
  and let not thy dread make me afraid.
Then call thou, and I will answer:
  or let me speak, and answer thou me.
How many are mine iniquities and sins?
  make me to know my transgression and my sin.
Wherefore hidest thou thy face,
  and holdest me for thine enemy?
Wilt thou break a leaf driven to and fro?
  and wilt thou pursue the dry stubble?
For thou writest bitter things against me,
  and makest me to possess the iniquities of my youth.
Thou puttest my feet also in the stocks,
  and lookest narrowly unto all my paths;
  thou settest a print upon the heels of my feet.

And he, as a rotten thing, consumeth,
  as a garment that is moth eaten.

Man that is born of a woman
  is of few days, and full of trouble.
He cometh forth like a flower, and is cut down:
  he fleeth also as a shadow, and continueth not.
And doth thou open thine eyes upon such an one,
  and bringest me into judgment with thee?

Who can bring a clean thing out of an unclean?
    not one.
Seeing his days are determined,
    the number of his months are with thee,
    thou hast appointed his bounds that he cannot pass;
Turn from him, that he may rest,
    till he shall accomplish, as an hireling, his day.

For there is hope of a tree, if it be cut down,
    that it will sprout again,
    and that the tender branch thereof will not cease.
Though the root thereof wax old in the earth,
    and the stock thereof die in the ground;
Yet through the scent of water it will bud,
    and bring forth boughs like a plant.
But man dieth, and wasteth away:
    yea, man giveth up the ghost, and where is he?
As the waters fail from the sea,
    and the flood decayeth and drieth up:
So man lieth down, and riseth not:
    till the heavens be no more, they shall not awake,
    nor be raised out of their sleep.

O that thou wouldest hide me in the grave,
    that thou wouldest keep me secret, until thy wrath be past,
that thou wouldest appoint me a set time,
    and remember me!
If a man die, shall he live again?
    all the days of my appointed time will I wait,
    till my change come.
Thou shalt call, and I will answer thee:
    thou wilt have a desire to the work of thine hands.
For now thou numberest my steps:
    dost thou not watch over my sin?
My transgression is sealed up in a bag,
    and thou sewest up mine iniquity.

And surely the mountains falling cometh to nought,
    and the rock is removed out of his place.
The waters wear the stones:
    thou washest away the things which grow out of the
        dust of the earth;
    and thou destroyest the hope of man.
Thou prevailest for ever against him, and he passeth:
    thou changest his countenance, and sendest him away.
His sons come to honour, and he knoweth it not;
    and they are brought low, but he perceiveth it not of them.
But his flesh upon him shall have pain,
    and his soul within him shall mourn.

Part Two
The Second Cycle of Speeches

Job 15:1 – 21:34

Eliphaz

Then answered Eliphaz the Temanite, and said,

> Should a wise man utter vain knowledge,
>> and fill his belly with the east wind?
> Should he reason with unprofitable talk?
>> or with speeches wherewith he can do no good?
> Yea, thou castest off fear,
>> and restrainest prayer before God.
> For thy mouth uttereth thine iniquity,
>> and thou choosest the tongue of the crafty.
> Thine own mouth condemneth thee, and not I:
>> yea, thine own lips testify against thee.

> Art thou the first man that was born?
>> or wast thou made before the hills?
> Hast thou heard the secret of God?
>> and dost thou restrain wisdom to thyself?
> What knowest thou, that we know not?
>> what understandest thou, which is not in us?
> With us are both the grayheaded and very aged men,
>> much elder than thy father.
> Are the consolations of God small with thee?
>> is there any secret thing with thee?
> Why doth thine heart carry thee away?
>> and what do thy eyes wink at,
> That thou turnest thy spirit against God,
>> and lettest such words go out of thy mouth?

What is man, that he should be clean?
    and he which is born of a woman, that he should be
        righteous?
Behold, he putteth no trust in his saints;
    yea, the heavens are not clean in his sight.
How much more abominable and filthy is man,
    which drinketh iniquity like water?

I will shew thee, hear me;
    and that which I have seen I will declare;
Which wise men have told from their fathers,
    and have not hid it:
Unto whom alone the earth was given,
    and no stranger passed among them.
The wicked man travaileth with pain all his days,
    and the number of years is hidden to the oppressor.
A dreadful sound is in his ears:
    in prosperity the destroyer shall come upon him.
He believeth not that he shall return out of darkness,
    and he is waited for of the sword.
He wandereth abroad for bread, saying, Where is it?
    he knoweth that the day of darkness is ready at his hand.
Trouble and anguish shall make him afraid;
    they shall prevail against him, as a king ready to the battle.
For he stretcheth out his hand against God,
    and strengtheneth himself against the Almighty.
He runneth upon him, even on his neck,
    upon the thick bosses of his bucklers:

Because he covereth his face with his fatness,
    and maketh collops of fat on his flanks.
And he dwelleth in desolate cities,
    and in houses which no man inhabiteth,
    which are ready to become heaps.
He shall not be rich, neither shall his substance continue,
    neither shall he prolong the perfection thereof upon
        the earth.

He shall not depart out of darkness;
    the flame shall dry up his branches,
    and by the breath of his mouth shall he go away.
Let not him that is deceived trust in vanity:
    for vanity shall be his recompence.
It shall be accomplished before his time,
    and his branch shall not be green.
He shall shake off his unripe grape as the vine,
    and shall cast off his flower as the olive.
For the congregation of hypocrites shall be desolate,
    and fire shall consume the tabernacles of bribery.
They conceive mischief, and bring forth vanity,
    and their belly prepareth deceit.

Job

Then Job answered and said,

I have heard many such things:
    miserable comforters are ye all.
Shall vain words have an end?
    or what emboldeneth thee that thou answerest?
I also could speak as ye do:
    if your soul were in my soul's stead,
I could heap up words against you,
    and shake mine head at you.
But I would strengthen you with my mouth,
    and the moving of my lips should assuage your grief.

Though I speak, my grief is not assuaged:
    and though I forbear, what am I eased?
But now he hath made me weary:
    thou hast made desolate all my company.
And thou hast filled me with wrinkles, which is a witness
        against me:
    and my leanness rising up in me beareth witness to my face.

He teareth me in his wrath, who hateth me:
    he gnasheth upon me with his teeth;
    mine enemy sharpeneth his eyes upon me.
They have gaped upon me with their mouth;
    they have smitten me upon the cheek reproachfully;
    they have gathered themselves together against me.
God hath delivered me to the ungodly,
    and turned me over into the hands of the wicked.
I was at ease, but he hath broken me asunder:
    he hath also taken me by my neck, and shaken me to pieces,
    and set me up for his mark.
His archers compass me round about,
    he cleaveth my reins asunder, and doth not spare;
    he poureth out my gall upon the ground.
He breaketh me with breach upon breach,
    he runneth upon me like a giant.

I have sewed sackcloth upon my skin,
    and defiled my horn in the dust.
My face is foul with weeping,
    and on my eyelids is the shadow of death;
Not for any injustice in mine hands:
    also my prayer is pure.

O earth, cover not thou my blood,
    and let my cry have no place.
Also now, behold, my witness is in heaven,
    and my record is on high.
My friends scorn me:
    but mine eye poureth out tears unto God.
O that one might plead for a man with God,
    as a man pleadeth for his neighbour!

When a few years are come,
    then I shall go the way whence I shall not return.
My breath is corrupt, my days are extinct,
    the graves are ready for me.
Are there not mockers with me?
    and doth not mine eye continue in their provocation?

Lay down now, put me in a surety with thee;
>who is he that will strike hands with me?
For thou hast hid their heart from understanding:
>therefore shalt thou not exalt them.
He that speaketh flattery to his friends,
>even the eyes of his children shall fail.

He hath made me also a byword of the people;
>and aforetime I was as a tabret.
Mine eye also is dim by reason of sorrow,
>and all my members are as a shadow.
Upright men shall be astonied at this,
>and the innocent shall stir up himself against the hypocrite.
The righteous also shall hold on his way,
>and he that hath clean hands shall be stronger and stronger.

But as for you all, do ye return, and come now:
>for I cannot find one wise man among you.
My days are past, my purposes are broken off,
>even the thoughts of my heart.
They change the night into day:
>the light is short because of darkness.
If I wait, the grave is mine house:
>I have made my bed in the darkness.
I have said to corruption, Thou art my father:
>to the worm, Thou art my mother, and my sister.
And where is now my hope?
>as for my hope, who shall see it?
They shall go down to the bars of the pit,
>when our rest together is in the dust.

Bildad

Then answered Bildad the Shuhite, and said,

How long will it be ere ye make an end of words?
>mark, and afterwards we will speak.
Wherefore are we counted as beasts,
>and reputed vile in your sight?

He teareth himself in his anger:
    shall the earth be forsaken for thee?
    and shall the rock be removed out of his place?

Yea, the light of the wicked shall be put out,
    and the spark of his fire shall not shine.
The light shall be dark in his tabernacle,
    and his candle shall be put out with him.
The steps of his strength shall be straitened,
    and his own counsel shall cast him down.
For he is cast into a net by his own feet,
    and he walketh upon a snare.
The gin shall take him by the heel,
    and the robber shall prevail against him.
The snare is laid for him in the ground,
    and a trap for him in the way.
Terrors shall make him afraid on every side,
    and shall drive him to his feet.
His strength shall be hungerbitten,
    and destruction shall be ready at his side.
It shall devour the strength of his skin:
    even the firstborn of death shall devour his strength.
His confidence shall be rooted out of his tabernacle,
    and it shall bring him to the king of terrors.
It shall dwell in his tabernacle, because it is none of his:
    brimstone shall be scattered upon his habitation.
His roots shall be dried up beneath,
    and above shall his branch be cut off.
His remembrance shall perish from the earth,
    and he shall have no name in the street.
He shall be driven from light into darkness,
    and chased out of the world.
He shall neither have son nor nephew among his people,
    nor any remaining in his dwellings.
They that come after him shall be astonied at his day,
    as they that went before were affrighted.
Surely such are the dwellings of the wicked,
    and this is the place of him that knoweth not God.

Job

Then Job answered and said,

> How long will ye vex my soul,
>> and break me in pieces with words?
> These ten times have ye reproached me:
>> ye are not ashamed that ye make yourselves strange to me.
> And be it indeed that I have erred,
>> mine error remaineth with myself.
> If indeed ye will magnify yourselves against me,
>> and plead against me my reproach:
> Know now that God hath overthrown me,
>> and hath compassed me with his net.

> Behold, I cry out of wrong, but I am not heard:
>> I cry aloud, but there is no judgment.
> He hath fenced up my way that I cannot pass,
>> and he hath set darkness in my paths.
> He hath stripped me of my glory,
>> and taken the crown from my head.
> He hath destroyed me on every side, and I am gone:
>> and mine hope hath he removed like a tree.
> He hath also kindled his wrath against me,
>> and he counteth me unto him as one of his enemies.
> His troops come together,
>> and raise up their way against me,
>> and encamp round about my tabernacle.

> He hath put my brethren far from me,
>> and mine acquaintance are verily estranged from me.
> My kinsfolk have failed,
>> and my familiar friends have forgotten me.
> They that dwell in mine house, and my maids, count me
>> for a stranger:
>> I am an alien in their sight.
> I called my servant, and he gave me no answer;
>> I intreated him with my mouth.

73

My breath is strange to my wife,
    though I intreated for the children's sake of mine own body.
Yea, young children despised me;
    I arose, and they spake against me.
All my inward friends abhorred me:
    and they whom I loved are turned against me.
My bone cleaveth to my skin and to my flesh,
    and I am escaped with the skin of my teeth.

Have pity upon me, have pity upon me, O ye my friends;
    for the hand of God hath touched me.
Why do ye persecute me as God,
    and are not satisfied with my flesh?

Oh that my words were now written!
    oh that they were printed in a book!
That they were graven with an iron pen and lead
    in the rock for ever!
For I know that my redeemer liveth,
    and that he shall stand at the latter day upon the earth:
And though after my skin worms destroy this body,
    yet in my flesh shall I see God:
Whom I shall see for myself,
    and mine eyes shall behold, and not another;
    though my reins be consumed within me.
But ye should say, Why persecute we him,
    seeing the root of the matter is found in me?
Be ye afraid of the sword:
    for wrath bringeth the punishments of the sword,
    that ye may know there is a judgment.

Zophar

Then answered Zophar the Naamathite, and said,

    Therefore do my thoughts cause me to answer,
        and for this I make haste.
    I have heard the check of my reproach,
        and the spirit of my understanding causeth me to answer.

Knowest thou not this of old,
　　since man was placed upon earth,
That the triumphing of the wicked is short,
　　and the joy of the hypocrite but for a moment?
Though his excellency mount up to the heavens,
　　and his head reach unto the clouds;
Yet he shall perish for ever like his own dung:
　　they which have seen him shall say, Where is he?
He shall fly away as a dream, and shall not be found:
　　yea, he shall be chased away as a vision of the night.
The eye also which saw him shall see him no more;
　　neither shall his place any more behold him.
His children shall seek to please the poor,
　　and his hands shall restore their goods.
His bones are full of the sin of his youth,
　　which shall lie down with him in the dust.

Though wickedness be sweet in his mouth,
　　though he hide it under his tongue;
Though he spare it, and forsake it not;
　　but keep it still within his mouth:
Yet his meat in his bowels is turned,
　　it is the gall of asps within him.
He hath swallowed down riches, and he shall vomit them
　　　up again:
　　God shall cast them out of his belly.
He shall suck the poison of asps:
　　the viper's tongue shall slay him.
He shall not see the rivers, the floods,
　　the brooks of honey and butter.
That which he laboured for shall he restore, and shall not
　　　swallow it down:
　　according to his substance shall the restitution be,
　　and he shall not rejoice therein.
Because he hath oppressed and hath forsaken the poor;
　　because he hath violently taken away an house which
　　　he builded not;

Surely he shall not feel quietness in his belly,
    he shall not save of that which he desired.
There shall none of his meat be left;
    therefore shall no man look for his goods.
In the fulness of his sufficiency he shall be in straits:
    every hand of the wicked shall come upon him.
When he is about to fill his belly,
    God shall cast the fury of his wrath upon him,
    and shall rain it upon him while he is eating.
He shall flee from the iron weapon,
    and the bow of steel shall strike him through.
It is drawn, and cometh out of the body;
    yea, the glittering sword cometh out of his gall:
    terrors are upon him.
All darkness shall be hid in his secret places:
    a fire not blown shall consume him;
    it shall go ill with him that is left in his tabernacle.
The heaven shall reveal his iniquity;
    and the earth shall rise up against him.
The increase of his house shall depart,
    and his goods shall flow away in the day of his wrath.
This is the portion of a wicked man from God,
    and the heritage appointed unto him by God.

Job

But Job answered and said,

Hear diligently my speech,
    and let this be your consolations.
Suffer me that I may speak;
    and after that I have spoken, mock on.

As for me, is my complaint to man?
    and if it were so, why should not my spirit be troubled?
Mark me, and be astonished,
    and lay your hand upon your mouth.

Even when I remember I am afraid,
    and trembling taketh hold on my flesh.
Wherefore do the wicked live,
    become old, yea, are mighty in power?
Their seed is established in their sight with them,
    and their offspring before their eyes.
Their houses are safe from fear,
    neither is the rod of God upon them.
Their bull gendereth, and faileth not;
    their cow calveth, and casteth not her calf.
They send forth their little ones like a flock,
    and their children dance.
They take the timbrel and harp,
    and rejoice at the sound of the organ.
They spend their days in wealth,
    and in a moment go down to the grave.
Therefore they say unto God, Depart from us;
    for we desire not the knowledge of thy ways.
What is the Almighty, that we should serve him?
    and what profit should we have, if we pray unto him?
Lo, their good is not in their hand:
    the counsel of the wicked is far from me.

How oft is the candle of the wicked put out!
    and how oft cometh their destruction upon them!
    God distributeth sorrows in his anger.
They are as stubble before the wind,
    and as chaff that the storm carrieth away.
God layeth up his iniquity for his children:
    he rewardeth him, and he shall know it.
His eyes shall see his destruction,
    and he shall drink of the wrath of the Almighty.
For what pleasure hath he in his house after him,
    when the number of his months is cut off in the midst?

Shall any teach God knowledge?
    seeing he judgeth those that are high.

One dieth in his full strength,
    being wholly at ease and quiet.
His breasts are full of milk,
    and his bones are moistened with marrow.
And another dieth in the bitterness of his soul,
    and never eateth with pleasure.
They shall lie down alike in the dust,
    and the worms shall cover them.

Behold, I know your thoughts,
    and the devices which ye wrongfully imagine against me.
For ye say, Where is the house of the prince?
    and where are the dwelling places of the wicked?
Have ye not asked them that go by the way?
    and do ye not know their tokens,
That the wicked is reserved to the day of destruction?
    they shall be brought forth to the day of wrath.
Who shall declare his way to his face?
    and who shall repay him what he hath done?
Yet shall he be brought to the grave,
    and shall remain in the tomb.
The clods of the valley shall be sweet unto him,
    and every man shall draw after him,
        as there are innumerable before him.

How then comfort ye me in vain,
    seeing in your answers there remaineth falsehood?

Part Three

The Third Cycle of Speeches

Job 22:1 – 31:40

Eliphaz

Then Eliphaz the Temanite answered and said,

> Can a man be profitable unto God,
>   as he that is wise may be profitable unto himself?
> Is it any pleasure to the Almighty, that thou art righteous?
>   or is it gain to him, that thou makest thy ways perfect?
>
> Will he reprove thee for fear of thee?
>   will he enter with thee into judgment?
> Is not thy wickedness great?
>   and thine iniquities infinite?
> For thou hast taken a pledge from thy brother for nought,
>   and stripped the naked of their clothing.
> Thou hast not given water to the weary to drink,
>   and thou hast withholden bread from the hungry.
> But as for the mighty man, he had the earth;
>   and the honourable man dwelt in it.
> Thou hast sent widows away empty,
>   and the arms of the fatherless have been broken.
> Therefore snares are round about thee,
>   and sudden fear troubleth thee;
> Or darkness, that thou canst not see;
>   and abundance of waters cover thee.
>
> Is not God in the height of heaven?
>   and behold the height of the stars, how high they are!
> And thou sayest, How doth God know?
>   can he judge through the dark cloud?

Thick clouds are a covering to him, that he seeth not;
   and he walketh in the circuit of heaven.
Hast thou marked the old way
   which wicked men have trodden?
Which were cut down out of time,
   whose foundation was overflown with a flood:
Which said unto God, Depart from us:
   and what can the Almighty do for them?
Yet he filled their houses with good things:
   but the counsel of the wicked is far from me.

The righteous see it, and are glad:
   and the innocent laugh them to scorn.
Whereas our substance is not cut down,
   but the remnant of them the fire consumeth.

Acquaint now thyself with him, and be at peace:
   thereby good shall come unto thee.
Receive, I pray thee, the law from his mouth,
   and lay up his words in thine heart.
If thou return to the Almighty, thou shalt be built up,
   thou shalt put away iniquity far from thy tabernacles.
Then shalt thou lay up gold as dust,
   and the gold of Ophir as the stones of the brooks.
Yea, the Almighty shall be thy defence,
   and thou shalt have plenty of silver.
For then shalt thou have thy delight in the Almighty,
   and shalt lift up thy face unto God.
Thou shalt make thy prayer unto him, and he shall hear thee,
   and thou shalt pay thy vows.
Thou shalt also decree a thing, and it shall be established
     unto thee:
   and the light shall shine upon thy ways.
When men are cast down, then thou shalt say,
     There is lifting up;
   and he shall save the humble person.
He shall deliver the island of the innocent:
   and it is delivered by the pureness of thine hands.

Job

Then Job answered and said,

> Even to day is my complaint bitter:
>> my stroke is heavier than my groaning.
> Oh that I knew where I might find him!
>> that I might come even to his seat!
> I would order my cause before him,
>> and fill my mouth with arguments.
> I would know the words which he would answer me,
>> and understand what he would say unto me.
> Will he plead against me with his great power?
>> No; but he would put strength in me.
> There the righteous might dispute with him;
>> so should I be delivered for ever from my judge.

> Behold, I go forward, but he is not there;
>> and backward, but I cannot perceive him:
> On the left hand, where he doth work, but I cannot
>> behold him:
>> he hideth himself on the right hand, that I cannot see him:
> But he knoweth the way that I take:
>> when he hath tried me, I shall come forth as gold.
> My foot hath held his steps,
>> his way have I kept, and not declined.
> Neither have I gone back from the commandment of his lips;
>> I have esteemed the words of his mouth more than my
>> necessary food.

> But he is in one mind, and who can turn him?
>> and what his soul desireth, even that he doeth.
> For he performeth the thing that is appointed for me:
>> and many such things are with him.
> Therefore am I troubled at his presence:
>> when I consider, I am afraid of him.
> For God maketh my heart soft,
>> and the Almighty troubleth me:

Because I was not cut off before the darkness,
    neither hath he covered the darkness from my face.

Why, seeing times are not hidden from the Almighty,
    do they that know him not see his days?
Some remove the landmarks;
    they violently take away flocks, and feed thereof.
They drive away the ass of the fatherless,
    they take the widow's ox for a pledge.
They turn the needy out of the way:
    the poor of the earth hide themselves together.
Behold, as wild asses in the desert, go they forth to their work;
    rising betimes for a prey:
    the wilderness yieldeth food for them and for their children.
They reap every one his corn in the field:
    and they gather the vintage of the wicked.
They cause the naked to lodge without clothing,
    that they have no covering in the cold.
They are wet with the showers of the mountains,
    and embrace the rock for want of a shelter.
They pluck the fatherless from the breast,
    and take a pledge of the poor.
They cause him to go naked without clothing,
    and they take away the sheaf from the hungry;
Which make oil within their walls,
    and tread their winepresses, and suffer thirst.
Men groan from out of the city,
    and the soul of the wounded crieth out:
    yet God layeth not folly to them.

They are of those that rebel against the light;
    they know not the ways thereof,
    nor abide in the paths thereof.
The murderer rising with the light killeth the poor and needy,
    and in the night is as a thief.
The eye also of the adulterer waiteth for the twilight,
    saying, No eye shall see me:
    and disguiseth his face.

In the dark they dig through houses,
  which they had marked for themselves in the daytime:
  they know not the light.
For the morning is to them even as the shadow of death:
  if one know them, they are in the terrors of the shadow
    of death.

He is swift as the waters;
  their portion is cursed in the earth:
  he beholdeth not the way of the vineyards.
Drought and heat consume the snow waters:
  so doth the grave those which have sinned.
The womb shall forget him;
  the worm shall feed sweetly on him;
he shall be no more remembered;
  and wickedness shall be broken as a tree.
He evil entreateth the barren that beareth not:
  and doeth not good to the widow.
He draweth also the mighty with his power:
  he riseth up, and no man is sure of life.
Though it be given him to be in safety, whereon he resteth;
  yet his eyes are upon their ways.
They are exalted for a little while, but are gone and
    brought low;
  they are taken out of the way as all other,
  and cut off as the tops of the ears of corn.

And if it be not so now, who will make me a liar,
  and make my speech nothing worth?

Bildad

Then answered Bildad the Shuhite, and said,

Dominion and fear are with him,
  he maketh peace in his high places.
Is there any number of his armies?
  and upon whom doth not his light arise?

How then can man be justified with God?
    or how can he be clean that is born of a woman?
Behold even to the moon, and it shineth not;
    yea, the stars are not pure in his sight.
How much less man, that is a worm?
    and the son of man, which is a worm?

Job

But Job answered and said,

How hast thou helped him that is without power?
    how savest thou the arm that hath no strength?
How hast thou counselled him that hath no wisdom?
    and how hast thou plentifully declared the thing as it is?
To whom hast thou uttered words?
    and whose spirit came from thee?

Dead things are formed from under the waters,
    and the inhabitants thereof.
Hell is naked before him,
    and destruction hath no covering.
He stretcheth out the north over the empty place,
    and hangeth the earth upon nothing.
He bindeth up the waters in his thick clouds;
    and the cloud is not rent under them.
He holdeth back the face of his throne,
    and spreadeth his cloud upon it.
He hath compassed the waters with bounds,
    until the day and night come to an end.
The pillars of heaven tremble
    and are astonished at his reproof.
He divideth the sea with his power,
    and by his understanding he smiteth through the proud.
By his spirit he hath garnished the heavens;
    his hand hath formed the crooked serpent.
Lo, these are parts of his ways:

but how little a portion is heard of him?
but the thunder of his power who can understand?

Moreover Job continued his parable, and said,

As God liveth, who hath taken away my judgment;
and the Almighty, who hath vexed my soul;
All the while my breath is in me,
and the spirit of God is in my nostrils;
My lips shall not speak wickedness,
nor my tongue utter deceit.
God forbid that I should justify you:
till I die I will not remove mine integrity from me.
My righteousness I hold fast, and will not let it go:
my heart shall not reproach me so long as I live.

Let mine enemy be as the wicked,
and he that riseth up against me as the unrighteous.
For what is the hope of the hypocrite, though he hath gained,
when God taketh away his soul?
Will God hear his cry
when trouble cometh upon him?
Will he delight himself in the Almighty?
will he always call upon God?

I will teach you by the hand of God:
that which is with the Almighty will I not conceal.
Behold, all ye yourselves have seen it;
why then are ye thus altogether vain?

This is the portion of a wicked man with God,
and the heritage of oppressors, which they shall receive
of the Almighty.
If his children be multiplied, it is for the sword:
and his offspring shall not be satisfied with bread.
Those that remain of him shall be buried in death:
and his widows shall not weep.
Though he heap up silver as the dust,
and prepare raiment as the clay;

He may prepare it, but the just shall put it on,
    and the innocent shall divide the silver.
He buildeth his house as a moth,
    and as a booth that the keeper maketh.
The rich man shall lie down, but he shall not be gathered:
    he openeth his eyes, and he is not.
Terrors take hold on him as waters,
    a tempest stealeth him away in the night.
The east wind carrieth him away, and he departeth:
    and as a storm hurleth him out of his place.
For God shall cast upon him, and not spare:
    he would fain flee out of his hand.
Men shall clap their hands at him,
    and shall hiss him out of his place.

A Hymn to Wisdom

Surely there is a vein for the silver,
    and a place for gold where they fine it.
Iron is taken out of the earth,
    and brass is molten out of the stone.
He setteth an end to darkness, and searcheth out
      all perfection:
    the stones of darkness, and the shadow of death.
The flood breaketh out from the inhabitant;
    even the waters forgotten of the foot:
    they are dried up, they are gone away from men.
As for the earth, out of it cometh bread:
    and under it is turned up as it were fire.
The stones of it are the place of sapphires:
    and it hath dust of gold.
There is a path which no fowl knoweth,
    and which the vulture's eye hath not seen:
The lion's whelps have not trodden it,
    nor the fierce lion passed by it.
He putteth forth his hand upon the rock;

he overturneth the mountains by the roots.
He cutteth out rivers among the rocks;
   and his eye seeth every precious thing.
He bindeth the floods from overflowing;
   and the thing that is hid bringeth he forth to light.
But where shall wisdom be found?
   and where is the place of understanding?
Man knoweth not the price thereof;
   neither is it found in the land of the living.
The depth saith, It is not in me:
   and the sea saith, It is not with me.
It cannot be gotten for gold,
   neither shall silver be weighed for the price thereof.
It cannot be valued with the gold of Ophir,
   with the precious onyx, or the sapphire.
The gold and the crystal cannot equal it:
   and the exchange of it shall not be for jewels of fine gold.
No mention shall be made of coral, or of pearls:
   for the price of wisdom is above rubies.
The topaz of Ethiopia shall not equal it,
   neither shall it be valued with pure gold.

Whence then cometh wisdom?
   and where is the place of understanding?
Seeing it is hid from the eyes of all living,
   and kept close from the fowls of the air.
Destruction and death say,
   We have heard the fame thereof with our ears.
God understandeth the way thereof,
   and he knoweth the place thereof.
For he looketh to the ends of the earth,
   and seeth under the whole heaven;
To make the weight for the winds;
   and he weigheth the waters by measure.
When he made a decree for the rain,
   and a way for the lightning of the thunder:
Then did he see it, and declare it;
   he prepared it, yea, and searched it out.

And unto man he said,
> Behold, the fear of the Lord, that is wisdom;
> and to depart from evil is understanding.

Job

Moreover Job continued his parable, and said,

> Oh that I were as in months past,
> as in the days when God preserved me;
> When his candle shined upon my head,
> and when by his light I walked through darkness;
> As I was in the days of my youth,
> when the secret of God was upon my tabernacle;
> When the Almighty was yet with me,
> when my children were about me;
> When I washed my steps with butter,
> and the rock poured me out rivers of oil;

> When I went out to the gate through the city,
> when I prepared my seat in the street!
> The young men saw me, and hid themselves:
> and the aged arose, and stood up.
> The princes refrained talking,
> and laid their hand on their mouth.
> The nobles held their peace,
> and their tongue cleaved to the roof of their mouth.
> When the ear heard me, then it blessed me;
> and when the eye saw me, it gave witness to me:
> Because I delivered the poor that cried,
> and the fatherless, and him that had none to help him.
> The blessing of him that was ready to perish came upon me:
> and I caused the widow's heart to sing for joy.
> I put on righteousness, and it clothed me:
> my judgment was as a robe and a diadem.
> I was eyes to the blind,
> and feet was I to the lame.

I was a father to the poor:
  and the cause which I knew not I searched out.
And I brake the jaws of the wicked,
  and plucked the spoil out of his teeth.

Then I said, I shall die in my nest,
  and I shall multiply my days as the sand.
My root was spread out by the waters,
  and the dew lay all night upon my branch.
My glory was fresh in me,
  and my bow was renewed in my hand.

Unto me men gave ear, and waited,
  and kept silence at my counsel.
After my words they spake not again;
  and my speech dropped upon them.
And they waited for me as for the rain;
  and they opened their mouth wide as for the latter rain.
If I laughed on them, they believed it not;
  and the light of my countenance they cast not down.
I chose out their way, and sat chief,
  and dwelt as a king in the army,
  as one that comforteth the mourners.

But now they that are younger than I have me in derision,
  whose fathers I would have disdained
  to have set with the dogs of my flock.
Yea, whereto might the strength of their hands profit me,
  in whom old age was perished?
For want and famine they were solitary;
  fleeing into the wilderness
  in former time desolate and waste.
Who cut up mallows by the bushes,
  and juniper roots for their meat.
They were driven forth from among men,
  (they cried after them as after a thief;)
To dwell in the cliffs of the valleys,
  in caves of the earth, and in the rocks.

Among the bushes they brayed;
    under the nettles they were gathered together.
They were children of fools, yea, children of base men:
    they were viler than the earth.

And now am I their song,
    yea, I am their byword.
They abhor me, they flee far from me,
    and spare not to spit in my face.
Because he hath loosed my cord, and afflicted me,
    they have also let loose the bridle before me.
Upon my right hand rise the youth;
    they push away my feet,
    and they raise up against me the ways of their destruction.
They mar my path,
    they set forward my calamity,
    they have no helper.
They came upon me as a wide breaking in of waters:
    in the desolation they rolled themselves upon me.
Terrors are turned upon me:
    they pursue my soul as the wind:
    and my welfare passeth away as a cloud.

And now my soul is poured out upon me;
    the days of affliction have taken hold upon me.
My bones are pierced in me in the night season:
    and my sinews take no rest.
By the great force of my disease is my garment changed:
    it bindeth me about as the collar of my coat.
He hath cast me into the mire,
    and I am become like dust and ashes.

I cry unto thee, and thou dost not hear me:
    I stand up, and thou regardest me not.
Thou art become cruel to me:
    with thy strong hand thou opposest thyself against me.
Thou liftest me up to the wind;
    thou causest me to ride upon it, and dissolvest my substance.

For I know that thou wilt bring me to death,
  and to the house appointed for all living.

Howbeit he will not stretch out his hand to the grave,
  though they cry in his destruction.
Did not I weep for him that was in trouble?
  was not my soul grieved for the poor?
When I looked for good, then evil came unto me:
  and when I waited for light, there came darkness.
My bowels boiled, and rested not:
  the days of affliction prevented me.
I went mourning without the sun:
  I stood up, and I cried in the congregation.
I am a brother to dragons,
  and a companion to owls.
My skin is black upon me,
  and my bones are burned with heat.
My harp also is turned to mourning,
  and my organ into the voice of them that weep.

I made a covenant with mine eyes;
  why then should I think upon a maid?
For what portion of God is there from above?
  and what inheritance of the Almighty from on high?
Is not destruction to the wicked?
  and a strange punishment to the workers of iniquity?
Doth not he see my ways,
  and count all my steps?

If I have walked with vanity,
  or if my foot hath hasted to deceit;
Let me be weighed in an even balance,
  that God may know mine integrity.
If my step hath turned out of the way,
  and mine heart walked after mine eyes,
  and if any blot hath cleaved to mine hands;
Then let me sow, and let another eat;
  yea, let my offspring be rooted out.

If mine heart have been deceived by a woman,
　　or if I have laid wait at my neighbour's door;
Then let my wife grind unto another,
　　and let others bow down upon her.
For this is an heinous crime;
　　yea, it is an iniquity to be punished by the judges.
For it is a fire that consumeth to destruction,
　　and would root out all mine increase.

If I did despise the cause of my manservant or of my
　　　maidservant,
　　when they contended with me;
What then shall I do when God riseth up?
　　and when he visiteth, what shall I answer him?
Did not he that made me in the womb make him?
　　and did not one fashion us in the womb?

If I have withheld the poor from their desire,
　　or have caused the eyes of the widow to fail;
Or have eaten my morsel myself alone,
　　and the fatherless hath not eaten thereof;
(For from my youth he was brought up with me, as with a father,
　　and I have guided her from my mother's womb;)
If I have seen any perish for want of clothing,
　　or any poor without covering;
If his loins have not blessed me,
　　and if he were not warmed with the fleece of my sheep;
If I have lifted up my hand against the fatherless,
　　when I saw my help in the gate:
Then let mine arm fall from my shoulder blade,
　　and mine arm be broken from the bone.
For destruction from God was a terror to me,
　　and by reason of his highness I could not endure.

If I have made gold my hope,
　　or have said to the fine gold, Thou art my confidence;
If I rejoiced because my wealth was great,
　　and because mine hand had gotten much;

If I beheld the sun when it shined,
   or the moon walking in brightness;
And my heart hath been secretly enticed,
   or my mouth hath kissed my hand:
This also were an iniquity to be punished by the judge:
   for I should have denied the God that is above.

If I rejoiced at the destruction of him that hated me,
   or lifted up myself when evil found him:
Neither have I suffered my mouth to sin
   by wishing a curse to his soul.
If the men of my tabernacle said not,
   Oh that we had of his flesh! we cannot be satisfied.
The stranger did not lodge in the street:
   but I opened my doors to the traveller.
If I covered my transgressions as Adam,
   by hiding mine iniquity in my bosom:
Did I fear a great multitude,
   or did the contempt of families terrify me,
   that I kept silence, and went not out of the door?

Oh that one would hear me!
   behold, my desire is, that the Almighty would answer me,
   and that mine adversary had written a book.
Surely I would take it upon my shoulder,
   and bind it as a crown to me.
I would declare unto him the number of my steps;
   as a prince would I go near unto him.

If my land cry against me,
   or that the furrows likewise thereof complain;
If I have eaten the fruits thereof without money,
   or have caused the owners thereof to lose their life:
Let thistles grow instead of wheat,
   and cockle instead of barley.

The words of Job are ended.

Part Four

The Speeches of Elihu

Job 32:1 – 37:24

Elihu

So these three men ceased to answer Job, because he was righteous in his own eyes. Then was kindled the wrath of Elihu the son of Barachel the Buzite, of the kindred of Ram: against Job was his wrath kindled, because he justified himself rather than God. Also against his three friends was his wrath kindled, because they had found no answer, and yet had condemned Job. Now Elihu had waited till Job had spoken, because they were elder than he. When Elihu saw that there was no answer in the mouth of these three men, then his wrath was kindled.

And Elihu the son of Barachel the Buzite answered and said,

I am young,
  and ye are very old;
wherefore I was afraid,
  and durst not shew you mine opinion.
I said, Days should speak,
  and multitude of years should teach wisdom.
But there is a spirit in man:
  and the inspiration of the Almighty giveth them
  understanding.
Great men are not always wise:
  neither do the aged understand judgment.

Therefore I said, Hearken to me;
  I also will shew mine opinion.
Behold, I waited for your words;
  I gave ear to your reasons,
  whilst ye searched out what to say.

Yea, I attended unto you,
    and, behold, there was none of you that convinced Job,
    or that answered his words:
Lest ye should say, We have found out wisdom:
    God thrusteth him down, not man.
Now he hath not directed his words against me:
    neither will I answer him with your speeches.

They were amazed, they answered no more:
    they left off speaking.
When I had waited, (for they spake not,
    but stood still, and answered no more;)
I said, I will answer also my part,
    I also will shew mine opinion.
For I am full of matter,
    the spirit within me constraineth me.
Behold, my belly is as wine which hath no vent;
    it is ready to burst like new bottles.
I will speak, that I may be refreshed:
    I will open my lips and answer.
Let me not, I pray you, accept any man's person,
    neither let me give flattering titles unto man.
For I know not to give flattering titles;
    in so doing my maker would soon take me away.

Wherefore, Job, I pray thee, hear my speeches,
    and hearken to all my words.
Behold, now I have opened my mouth,
    my tongue hath spoken in my mouth.
My words shall be of the uprightness of my heart:
    and my lips shall utter knowledge clearly.
The spirit of God hath made me,
    and the breath of the Almighty hath given me life.
If thou canst answer me,
    set thy words in order before me, stand up.
Behold, I am according to thy wish in God's stead:
    I also am formed out of the clay.

Behold, my terror shall not make thee afraid,
    neither shall my hand be heavy upon thee.

Surely thou hast spoken in mine hearing,
    and I have heard the voice of thy words, saying,
I am clean without transgression, I am innocent;
    neither is there iniquity in me.
Behold, he findeth occasions against me,
    he counteth me for his enemy,
He putteth my feet in the stocks,
    he marketh all my paths.
Behold, in this thou art not just:
    I will answer thee, that God is greater than man.
Why dost thou strive against him?
    for he giveth not account of any of his matters.
For God speaketh once, yea twice,
    yet man perceiveth it not.
In a dream, in a vision of the night,
    when deep sleep falleth upon men,
    in slumberings upon the bed;
Then he openeth the ears of men,
    and sealeth their instruction,
That he may withdraw man from his purpose,
    and hide pride from man.
He keepeth back his soul from the pit,
    and his life from perishing by the sword.
He is chastened also with pain upon his bed,
    and the multitude of his bones with strong pain:
So that his life abhorreth bread,
    and his soul dainty meat.
His flesh is consumed away, that it cannot be seen;
    and his bones that were not seen stick out.
Yea, his soul draweth near unto the grave,
    and his life to the destroyers.

If there be a messenger with him,
    an interpreter, one among a thousand,
    to shew unto man his uprightness:

Then he is gracious unto him, and saith,
   Deliver him from going down to the pit:
   I have found a ransom.
His flesh shall be fresher than a child's:
   he shall return to the days of his youth:
He shall pray unto God, and he will be favourable unto him:
   and he shall see his face with joy:
   for he will render unto man his righteousness.
He looketh upon men, and if any say,
   I have sinned, and perverted that which was right,
   and it profited me not;
He will deliver his soul from going into the pit,
   and his life shall see the light.

Lo, all these things worketh God
   oftentimes with man,
To bring back his soul from the pit,
   to be enlightened with the light of the living.

Mark well, O Job, hearken unto me:
   hold thy peace, and I will speak.
If thou hast anything to say, answer me:
   speak, for I desire to justify thee.
If not, hearken unto me:
   hold thy peace, and I shall teach thee wisdom.

Furthermore Elihu answered and said,

Hear my words, O ye wise men;
   and give ear unto me, ye that have knowledge.
For the ear trieth words,
   as the mouth tasteth meat.
Let us choose to us judgment:
   let us know among ourselves what is good.

For Job hath said, I am righteous:
   and God hath taken away my judgment.
Should I lie against my right?
   my wound is incurable without transgression.
What man is like Job,
   who drinketh up scorning like water?

Which goeth in company with the workers of iniquity,
   and walketh with wicked men.
For he hath said, It profiteth a man nothing
   that he should delight himself with God.

Therefore hearken unto me, ye men of understanding:
   far be it from God, that he should do wickedness;
   and from the Almighty, that he should commit iniquity.
For the work of a man shall he render unto him,
   and cause every man to find according to his ways.
Yea, surely God will not do wickedly,
   neither will the Almighty pervert judgment.
Who hath given him a charge over the earth?
   or who hath disposed the whole world?
If he set his heart upon man,
   if he gather unto himself his spirit and his breath;
All flesh shall perish together,
   and man shall turn again unto dust.

If now thou hast understanding, hear this:
   hearken to the voice of my words.
Shall even he that hateth right govern?
   and wilt thou condemn him that is most just?
Is it fit to say to a king, Thou art wicked?
   and to princes, Ye are ungodly?
How much less to him that accepteth not the persons
     of princes,
   nor regardeth the rich more than the poor?
   for they all are the work of his hands.
In a moment shall they die,
   and the people shall be troubled at midnight,
     and pass away:
   and the mighty shall be taken away without hand.

For his eyes are upon the ways of man,
   and he seeth all his goings.
There is no darkness, nor shadow of death,
   where the workers of iniquity may hide themselves.
For he will not lay upon man more than right;
   that he should enter into judgment with God.

He shall break in pieces mighty men without number,
    and set others in their stead.
Therefore he knoweth their works,
    and he overturneth them in the night, so that they
        are destroyed.
He striketh them as wicked men
    in the open sight of others;
Because they turned back from him,
    and would not consider any of his ways:
So that they cause the cry of the poor to come unto him,
    and he heareth the cry of the afflicted.
When he giveth quietness, who then can make trouble?
    and when he hideth his face, who then can behold him?
    whether it be done against a nation, or against a man only:
That the hypocrite reign not,
    lest the people be ensnared.

Surely it is meet to be said unto God,
    I have borne chastisement, I will not offend any more:
That which I see not teach thou me:
    if I have done iniquity, I will do no more.
Should it be according to thy mind? he will recompense it,
    whether thou refuse, or whether thou choose; and not I:
    therefore speak what thou knowest.
Let men of understanding tell me,
    and let a wise man hearken unto me.
Job hath spoken without knowledge,
    and his words were without wisdom.
My desire is that Job may be tried unto the end
    because of his answers for wicked men.
For he addeth rebellion unto his sin,
    he clappeth his hands among us,
    and multiplieth his words against God.

Elihu spake moreover, and said,

    Thinkest thou this to be right, that thou saidst,
        My righteousness is more than God's?

For thou saidst, What advantage will it be unto thee? and,
    What profit shall I have, if I be cleansed from my sin?

I will answer thee,
    and thy companions with thee.
Look unto the heavens, and see;
    and behold the clouds which are higher than thou.
If thou sinnest, what doest thou against him?
    or if thy transgressions be multiplied, what doest thou
        unto him?
If thou be righteous, what givest thou him?
    or what receiveth he of thine hand?
Thy wickedness may hurt a man as thou art;
    and thy righteousness may profit the son of man.

By reason of the multitude of oppressions they make
        the oppressed to cry:
    they cry out by reason of the arm of the mighty.
But none saith, Where is God my maker,
    who giveth songs in the night;
Who teacheth us more than the beasts of the earth,
    and maketh us wiser than the fowls of heaven?
There they cry, but none giveth answer,
    because of the pride of evil men.
Surely God will not hear vanity,
    neither will the Almighty regard it.
Although thou sayest thou shalt not see him,
    yet judgment is before him; therefore trust thou in him.
But now, because it is not so, he hath visited in his anger;
    yet he knoweth it not in great extremity:
Therefore doth Job open his mouth in vain;
    he multiplieth words without knowledge.

Elihu also proceeded, and said,

Suffer me a little, and I will shew thee
    that I have yet to speak on God's behalf.
I will fetch my knowledge from afar,
    and will ascribe righteousness to my Maker.

For truly my words shall not be false:
> he that is perfect in knowledge is with thee.

Behold, God is mighty, and despiseth not any:
> he is mighty in strength and wisdom.

He preserveth not the life of the wicked:
> but giveth right to the poor.

He withdraweth not his eyes from the righteous:
> but with kings are they on the throne;
> yea, he doth establish them for ever, and they are exalted.

And if they be bound in fetters,
> and be holden in cords of affliction;

Then he sheweth them their work,
> and their transgressions that they have exceeded.

He openeth also their ear to discipline,
> and commandeth that they return from iniquity.

If they obey and serve him,
> they shall spend their days in prosperity,
> and their years in pleasures.

But if they obey not,
> they shall perish by the sword,
> and they shall die without knowledge.

But the hypocrites in heart heap up wrath:
> they cry not when he bindeth them.

They die in youth,
> and their life is among the unclean.

He delivereth the poor in his affliction,
> and openeth their ears in oppression.

Even so would he have removed thee out of the strait
> into a broad place, where there is no straitness;
> and that which should be set on thy table should be full
> of fatness.

But thou hast fulfilled the judgment of the wicked:
> judgment and justice take hold on thee.

Because there is wrath, beware lest he take thee away with
> his stroke:
> then a great ransom cannot deliver thee.

Will he esteem thy riches?
    no, not gold, nor all the forces of strength.
Desire not the night,
    when people are cut off in their place.
Take heed, regard not iniquity:
    for this hast thou chosen rather than affliction.

Behold, God exalteth by his power:
    who teacheth like him?
Who hath enjoined him his way?
    or who can say, Thou hast wrought iniquity?
Remember that thou magnify his work,
    which men behold.
Every man may see it;
    man may behold it afar off.
Behold, God is great, and we know him not,
    neither can the number of his years be searched out.
For he maketh small the drops of water:
    they pour down rain according to the vapour thereof:
Which the clouds do drop
    and distil upon man abundantly.

Also can any understand the spreadings of the clouds,
    or the noise of his tabernacle?
Behold, he spreadeth his light upon it,
    and covereth the bottom of the sea.
For by them judgeth he the people;
    he giveth meat in abundance.
With clouds he covereth the light;
    and commandeth it not to shine by the cloud that
        cometh betwixt.
The noise thereof sheweth concerning it,
    the cattle also concerning the vapour.

At this also my heart trembleth,
    and is moved out of his place.
Hear attentively the noise of his voice,
    and the sound that goeth out of his mouth.

He directeth it under the whole heaven,
  and his lightning unto the ends of the earth.
After it a voice roareth:
  he thundereth with the voice of his excellency;
  and he will not stay them when his voice is heard.
God thundereth marvellously with his voice;
  great things doeth he, which we cannot comprehend.
For he saith to the snow, Be thou on the earth;
  likewise to the small rain, and to the great rain of his strength.
He sealeth up the hand of every man;
  that all men may know his work.
Then the beasts go into dens,
  and remain in their places.
Out of the south cometh the whirlwind:
  and cold out of the north.
By the breath of God frost is given:
  and the breadth of the waters is straitened.
Also by watering he wearieth the thick cloud:
  he scattereth his bright cloud:
And it is turned round about by his counsels:
  that they may do whatsoever he commandeth them
  upon the face of the world in the earth.
He causeth it to come, whether for correction,
  or for his land, or for mercy.

Hearken unto this, O Job:
  stand still, and consider the wondrous works of God.
Dost thou know when God disposed them,
  and caused the light of his cloud to shine?
Dost thou know the balancings of the clouds,
  the wondrous works of him which is perfect in knowledge?
How thy garments are warm,
  when he quieteth the earth by the south wind?
Hast thou with him spread out the sky,
  which is strong, and as a molten looking glass?

Teach us what we shall say unto him;
  for we cannot order our speech by reason of darkness.

Shall it be told him that I speak?
    if a man speak, surely he shall be swallowed up.
And now men see not the bright light which is in the clouds:
    but the wind passeth, and cleanseth them.
Fair weather cometh out of the north:
    with God is terrible majesty.
Touching the Almighty, we cannot find him out: he is
        excellent in power,
    and in judgment, and in plenty of justice: he will not afflict.
Men do therefore fear him:
    he respecteth not any that are wise of heart.

Part Five

The Speeches of Yahweh

Job 38:1 – 42:6

The Lord

Then the Lord answered Job out of the whirlwind, and said,

> Who is this that darkeneth counsel
> by words without knowledge?
> Gird up now thy loins like a man;
> for I will demand of thee,
> and answer thou me.
>
> Where wast thou when I laid the foundations of the earth?
> declare, if thou hast understanding.
> Who hath laid the measures thereof, if thou knowest?
> or who hath stretched the line upon it?
> Whereupon are the foundations thereof fastened?
> or who laid the corner stone thereof;
> When the morning stars sang together,
> and all the sons of God shouted for joy?
>
> Or who shut up the sea with doors,
> when it brake forth, as if it had issued out of the womb?
> When I made the cloud the garment thereof,
> and thick darkness a swaddlingband for it,
> And brake up for it my decreed place,
> and set bars and doors,
> And said, Hitherto shalt thou come, but no further:
> and here shall thy proud waves be stayed?
>
> Hast thou commanded the morning since thy days;
> and caused the dayspring to know his place;

That it might take hold of the ends of the earth,
    that the wicked might be shaken out of it?
It is turned as clay to the seal;
    and they stand as a garment.
And from the wicked their light is withholden,
    and the high arm shall be broken.

Hast thou entered into the springs of the sea?
    or hast thou walked in the search of the depth?
Have the gates of death been opened unto thee?
    or hast thou seen the doors of the shadow of death?
Hast thou perceived the breadth of the earth?
    declare if thou knowest it all.

Where is the way where light dwelleth?
    and as for darkness, where is the place thereof,
That thou shouldest take it to the bound thereof,
    and that thou shouldest know the paths to the house
        thereof?
Knowest thou it, because thou wast then born?
    or because the number of thy days is great?

Hast thou entered into the treasures of the snow?
    or hast thou seen the treasures of the hail,
Which I have reserved against the time of trouble,
    against the day of battle and war?
By what way is the light parted,
    which scattereth the east wind upon the earth?
Who hath divided a watercourse for the overflowing of waters,
    or a way for the lightning of thunder;
To cause it to rain on the earth, where no man is;
    on the wilderness, wherein there is no man;
To satisfy the desolate and waste ground;
    and to cause the bud of the tender herb to spring forth?
Hath the rain a father?
    or who hath begotten the drops of dew?
Out of whose womb came the ice?
    and the hoary frost of heaven, who hath gendered it?

The waters are hid as with a stone,
and the face of the deep is frozen.

Canst thou bind the sweet influences of Pleiades,
or loose the bands of Orion?
Canst thou bring forth Mazzaroth in his season?
or canst thou guide Arcturus with his sons?
Knowest thou the ordinances of heaven?
canst thou set the dominion thereof in the earth?

Canst thou lift up thy voice to the clouds,
that abundance of waters may cover thee?
Canst thou send lightnings,
that they may go, and say unto thee, Here we are?
Who hath put wisdom in the inward parts?
or who hath given understanding to the heart?
Who can number the clouds in wisdom?
or who can stay the bottles of heaven,
When the dust groweth into hardness,
and the clods cleave fast together?

Wilt thou hunt the prey for the lion?
or fill the appetite of the young lions,
When they couch in their dens,
and abide in the covert to lie in wait?
Who provideth for the raven his food?
when his young ones cry unto God,
they wander for lack of meat.

Knowest thou the time when the wild goats of the rock
bring forth?
or canst thou mark when the hinds do calve?
Canst thou number the months that they fulfil?
or knowest thou the time when they bring forth?
They bow themselves, they bring forth their young ones,
they cast out their sorrows.
Their young ones are in good liking, they grow up with corn;
they go forth, and return not unto them.

Who hath sent out the wild ass free?
  or who hath loosed the bands of the wild ass?
Whose house I have made the wilderness,
  and the barren land his dwellings.
He scorneth the multitude of the city,
  neither regardeth he the crying of the driver.
The range of the mountains is his pasture,
  and he searcheth after every green thing.

Will the unicorn be willing to serve thee,
  or abide by thy crib?
Canst thou bind the unicorn with his band in the furrow?
  or will he harrow the valleys after thee?
Wilt thou trust him, because his strength is great?
  or wilt thou leave thy labour to him?
Wilt thou believe him, that he will bring home thy seed,
  and gather it into thy barn?

Gavest thou the goodly wings unto the peacocks?
  or wings and feathers unto the ostrich?
Which leaveth her eggs in the earth,
  and warmeth them in dust,
And forgetteth that the foot may crush them,
  or that the wild beast may break them.
She is hardened against her young ones,
  as though they were not hers: her labour is in vain
    without fear;
Because God hath deprived her of wisdom,
  neither hath he imparted to her understanding.
What time she lifteth up herself on high,
  she scorneth the horse and his rider.

Hast thou given the horse strength?
  hast thou clothed his neck with thunder?
Canst thou make him afraid as a grasshopper?
  the glory of his nostrils is terrible.
He paweth in the valley, and rejoiceth in his strength:
  he goeth on to meet the armed men.

He mocketh at fear, and is not affrighted;
  neither turneth he back from the sword.
The quiver rattleth against him,
  the glittering spear and the shield.
He swalloweth the ground with fierceness and rage:
  neither believeth he that it is the sound of the trumpet.
He saith among the trumpets, Ha, ha;
  and he smelleth the battle afar off,
  the thunder of the captains, and the shouting.

Doth the hawk fly by thy wisdom,
  and stretch her wings toward the south?
Doth the eagle mount up at thy command,
  and make her nest on high?
She dwelleth and abideth on the rock,
  upon the crag of the rock, and the strong place.
From thence she seeketh the prey,
  and her eyes behold afar off.
Her young ones also suck up blood:
  and where the slain are, there is she.

Moreover the Lord answered Job, and said,

  Shall he that contendeth with the Almighty instruct him?
    he that reproveth God, let him answer it.

Then Job answered the Lord, and said,

  Behold, I am vile; what shall I answer thee?
    I will lay mine hand upon my mouth.
  Once have I spoken; but I will not answer:
    yea, twice; but I will proceed no further.

Then answered the Lord unto Job out of the whirlwind, and said,

  Gird up thy loins now like a man:
    I will demand of thee,
    and declare thou unto me.

  Wilt thou also disannul my judgment?
    wilt thou condemn me, that thou mayest be righteous?

111

Hast thou an arm like God?
 or canst thou thunder with a voice like him?
Deck thyself now with majesty and excellency;
 and array thyself with glory and beauty.
Cast abroad the rage of thy wrath:
 and behold every one that is proud, and abase him.
Look on every one that is proud, and bring him low;
 and tread down the wicked in their place.
Hide them in the dust together;
 and bind their faces in secret.
Then will I also confess unto thee
 that thine own right hand can save thee.
Behold now behemoth,
 which I made with thee;
 he eateth grass as an ox.
Lo now, his strength is in his loins,
 and his force is in the navel of his belly.
He moveth his tail like a cedar:
 the sinews of his stones are wrapped together.
His bones are as strong pieces of brass;
 his bones are like bars of iron.
He is the chief of the ways of God:
 he that made him can make his sword to approach
  unto him.
Surely the mountains bring him forth food,
 where all the beasts of the field play.
He lieth under the shady trees,
 in the covert of the reed, and fens.
The shady trees cover him with their shadow;
 the willows of the brook compass him about.
Behold, he drinketh up a river, and hasteth not:
 he trusteth that he can draw up Jordan into his mouth.
He taketh it with his eyes:
 his nose pierceth through snares.

Canst thou draw out leviathan with an hook?
 or his tongue with a cord which thou lettest down?

Canst thou put an hook into his nose?
  or bore his jaw through with a thorn?
Will he make many supplications unto thee?
  will he speak soft words unto thee?
Will he make a covenant with thee?
  wilt thou take him for a servant for ever?
Wilt thou play with him as with a bird?
  or wilt thou bind him for thy maidens?
Shall the companions make a banquet of him?
  shall they part him among the merchants?
Canst thou fill his skin with barbed irons?
  or his head with fish spears?
Lay thine hand upon him,
  remember the battle, do no more.
Behold, the hope of him is in vain:
  shall not one be cast down even at the sight of him?
None is so fierce that dare stir him up:
  who then is able to stand before me?
Who hath prevented me, that I should repay him?
  whatsoever is under the whole heaven is mine.

I will not conceal his parts,
  nor his power, nor his comely proportion.
Who can discover the face of his garment?
  or who can come to him with his double bridle?
Who can open the doors of his face?
  his teeth are terrible round about.
His scales are his pride,
  shut up together as with a close seal.
One is so near to another,
  that no air can come between them.
They are joined one to another,
  they stick together, that they cannot be sundered.
By his neesings a light doth shine,
  and his eyes are like the eyelids of the morning.
Out of his mouth go burning lamps,
  and sparks of fire leap out.

Out of his nostrils goeth smoke,
    as out of a seething pot or caldron.
His breath kindleth coals,
    and a flame goeth out of his mouth.
In his neck remaineth strength,
    and sorrow is turned into joy before him.
The flakes of his flesh are joined together:
    they are firm in themselves; they cannot be moved.
His heart is as firm as a stone;
    yea, as hard as a piece of the nether millstone.
When he raiseth up himself, the mighty are afraid:
    by reason of breakings they purify themselves.
The sword of him that layeth at him cannot hold:
    the spear, the dart, nor the habergeon.
He esteemeth iron as straw,
    and brass as rotten wood.
The arrow cannot make him flee:
    slingstones are turned with him into stubble.
Darts are counted as stubble:
    he laugheth at the shaking of a spear.
Sharp stones are under him:
    he spreadeth sharp pointed things upon the mire.
He maketh the deep to boil like a pot:
    he maketh the sea like a pot of ointment.
He maketh a path to shine after him;
    one would think the deep to be hoary.
Upon earth there is not his like,
    who is made without fear.
He beholdeth all high things:
    he is a king over all the children of pride.

Job

Then Job answered the Lord, and said,

    I know that thou canst do every thing,
        and that no thought can be withholden from thee.

Who is he that hideth counsel without knowledge?
   therefore have I uttered that I understood not;
   things too wonderful for me, which I knew not.

Hear, I beseech thee, and I will speak:
   I will demand of thee, and declare thou unto me.
I have heard of thee by the hearing of the ear:
   but now mine eye seeth thee.
Wherefore I abhor myself,
   and repent in dust and ashes.

Epilogue
Job's Reward

Job 42:7–17

And it was so, that after the Lord had spoken these words unto Job, the Lord said to Eliphaz the Temanite, My wrath is kindled against thee, and against thy two friends: for ye have not spoken of me the thing that is right, as my servant Job hath. Therefore take unto you now seven bullocks and seven rams, and go to my servant Job, and offer up for yourselves a burnt offering; and my servant Job shall pray for you: for him will I accept: lest I deal with you after your folly, in that ye have not spoken of me the thing which is right, like my servant Job. So Eliphaz the Temanite and Bildad the Shuhite and Zophar the Naamathite went, and did according as the Lord commanded them: the Lord also accepted Job.

And the Lord turned the captivity of Job, when he prayed for his friends: also the Lord gave Job twice as much as he had before. Then came there unto him all his brethren, and all his sisters, and all they that had been of his acquaintance before, and did eat bread with him in his house: and they bemoaned him, and comforted him over all the evil that the Lord had brought upon him: every man also gave him a piece of money, and every one an earring of gold.

So the Lord blessed the latter end of Job more than his beginning: for he had fourteen thousand sheep, and six thousand camels, and a thousand yoke of oxen, and a thousand she asses. He had also seven sons and three daughters. And he called the name of the first, Jemima; and the name of the second, Kezia; and the name of the third, Kerenhappuch. And in all the land were no women found so fair as the daughters of Job: and their father gave them inheritance among their brethren.

After this lived Job an hundred and forty years, and saw his sons, and his sons' sons, even four generations. So Job died, being old and full of days.

Index of Primary Sources